The Power of Distraction

Also Available from Bloomsbury

Maine de Biran's "Of Immediate Apperception,"
Maine de Biran Ed. Alessandra Aloisi, Marco Piazza, and Mark Sinclair, trans. Mark Sinclair
Joy and Laughter in Nietzsche's Philosophy,
Ed. Paul E. Kirkland and Michael J. McNeal
Encounters in the Arts, Literature, and Philosophy,
Ed. Jérôme Brillaud and Virginie Greene
The Poetics of Sleep, Simon Morgan Wortham

Expanded edition of *La potenza della distrazione*, originally published in Italian. Copyright © 2020 by Società editrice il Mulino, Bologna.

The Power of Distraction

Diversion and Reverie from Montaigne to Proust

Alessandra Aloisi

BLOOMSBURY ACADEMIC
LONDON • NEW YORK • OXFORD • NEW DELHI • SYDNEY

BLOOMSBURY ACADEMIC
Bloomsbury Publishing Plc
50 Bedford Square, London, WC1B 3DP, UK
1385 Broadway, New York, NY 10018, USA
29 Earlsfort Terrace, Dublin 2, Ireland

BLOOMSBURY, BLOOMSBURY ACADEMIC and the Diana logo are trademarks of Bloomsbury Publishing Plc

First published in Great Britain 2023
This paperback edition published in 2025

Copyright © Alessandra Aloisi, 2023

Alessandra Aloisi has asserted her right under the Copyright, Designs and Patents Act, 1988, to be identified as Author of this work.

Series design by Charlotte Daniels
Cover image: Gustave Courbet, The Wave (La Vague), 1869–1870, Oil on canvas, (© incamerastock / Alamy Stock Photo) (CC BY-NC)

All rights reserved. No part of this publication may be reproduced or transmitted in any form or by any means, electronic or mechanical, including photocopying, recording, or any information storage or retrieval system, without prior permission in writing from the publishers.

Bloomsbury Publishing Plc does not have any control over, or responsibility for, any third-party websites referred to or in this book. All internet addresses given in this book were correct at the time of going to press. The author and publisher regret any inconvenience caused if addresses have changed or sites have ceased to exist, but can accept no responsibility for any such changes.

A catalogue record for this book is available from the British Library.

Library of Congress Cataloging-in-Publication Data
Names: Aloisi, Alessandra, author.
Title: The power of distraction : diversion and reverie from Montaigne to Proust / Alessandra Aloisi.
Description: London ; New York : Bloomsbury Academic, 2023. | Includes bibliographical references and index.
Identifiers: LCCN 2023022758 (print) | LCCN 2023022759 (ebook) | ISBN 9781350342941 (hb) | ISBN 9781350342989 (pb) | ISBN 9781350342958 (epdf) | ISBN 9781350342965 (ebook)
Subjects: LCSH: Distraction (Philosophy)
Classification: LCC B105.D58 A46 2023 (print) | LCC B105.D58 (ebook) | DDC 128/.3–dc23/eng/20230710
LC record available at https://lccn.loc.gov/2023022758
LC ebook record available at https://lccn.loc.gov/2023022759

ISBN:	HB:	978-1-3503-4294-1
	PB:	978-1-3503-4298-9
	ePDF:	978-1-3503-4295-8
	eBook:	978-1-3503-4296-5

Typeset by Integra Software Services Pvt. Ltd.

To find out more about our authors and books visit www.bloomsbury.com and sign up for our newsletters.

To Angelina

*Selon moy, ce ne sont que mousches et atomes
qui promeinent ma volonté.*
Montaigne, *Essais*, III, 2

*Il faut écrire liquide ou gazeux, justement parce que la perception et
l'opinion ordinaires sont solides, géométriques.*
Gilles Deleuze, *Pourparlers*

Contents

Foreword · xi

Introduction to the English Edition · 1
Introduction to the Italian Edition · 13

Part 1 Divertissement
Avant-propos

1. Montaigne and Pascal, or the Difference between Ethics and Morality · 24
2. The "Sublime Misanthropist": Voltaire against Pascal · 28
3. One Man Alone in a Room · 32
4. Maine de Biran Criticizing (Voltaire Criticizing) Pascal · 39
5. Assault on the "Inner Citadel" · 43
6. Chasing a Hare: Pascal on the Unpleasant Use of Pleasure · 47
7. The "Theory of Pleasure": Leopardi between Pascal and Montaigne · 51

Part 2 The Power of Flies
Avant-propos

1. Augustine and Pascal · 57
2. Serendipity · 61
3. A Distracted Mathematician: Poincaré and the Role of Distraction in Invention · 63
4. Distraction and Trains of Thought: Locke and the Lesson of Sensationism · 68

5. What Is Essential Is (Not) Invisible to the Eye: Proust, Distraction, and Signs	74
6. Involuntary Memory	84
7. The Spider and the Connoisseur: On Art, Literary Vocation, and Jealousy	86
8. "The Entire History of You"	90

Part 3   Rêverie
Avant-propos

1. Dreams, Reveries, Fantasies	96
2. Reverie and Childhood: On Sand, Proust, and Flaubert	99
3. Travel, Motion, Solitude: Rousseau and the Pleasures of Reverie	103
4. Distraction and Automatism: *le moi d'habitude* and *le moi de réflexion*	109
5. The "System of the Soul and the Beast" or the Dangers of Distraction	113
6. Distraction and Somnambulism	118
7. Reverie and the History of Madness	123
8. Madness, Distraction, and Common Sense: On the Political and Aesthetic Dimension of Distraction and Reverie	126
9. Distraction and Idleness	131
Conclusion: Distraction and Laughter	135
Notes	139
Bibliography	173
Index	186

Foreword

Two years after the publication of this book in Italian in 2020, the English edition has given me the opportunity of supplementing my work with additional considerations and reflections here and there in the text and in a new introduction, specifically geared toward an English-speaking audience. This new introduction completes the introduction to the Italian edition. These new reflections, which do not change but rather reinforce and clarify the theses of the book, are not entirely removed from what has happened around us in these three years. This expanded edition has also been enriched by the generous remarks that I received on the occasion of the Italian and Spanish publications of this volume and its discussion in various contexts, in particular in the UCL French and Comparative Literature Research Seminar Series, the Seminar Series organized by the Laboratorio Nuova Buonarroti, Florence ("gli incontri di Quinto Alto"), the seminars of the Laboratorio Leopardi (Università di Roma La Sapienza), and the conference "Failure Is Our Best Option. The Politics of Literature and the Question of Reading" (Dartmouth College, Hanover, NH). I would like to thank Rachel Bowlby, Jennifer Rushworth, Alison Finch, Enrico Campo, Antonio Prete, Elena Sofia Arpe, Vincenzo Allegrini, Corrado Bologna, Jonathan Strauss, Jacques-David Ebguy, and Liesl Yamaguchi for the valuable observations and comments I received on these occasions. Vital inputs also came from my colleagues at Oxford, Kathryn Murphy and Nicholas Gaskill, with whom I have discussed attention and distraction on several occasions.

    A special thanks also goes to those who, in different contexts and in different ways, have helped, supported, or encouraged the first draft of this book: Katherine Astbury, Patrick Bray, Olmo Calzolari, Fabio Camilletti, Paola Cori, Franco D'Intino, Paolo Godani, Massimo

Mori, Marco Piazza, Valentina Tibaldo, and Caroline Warman. I also wish to thank my students for the invaluable opportunity to discuss, at a crucial stage of my work, many of the ideas which found their place in this book. This book was part of a research project that was generously funded by a Marie Curie research fellowship and hosted by the University of Warwick.

A first draft of the translation of this text was made by Sarah de Sanctis, whom I warmly thank for her work. For the assistance with the revision of the subsequent versions I wish to thank the friends and colleagues who have patiently reread this manuscript.

Unless otherwise indicated, the English translation of the passages cited in the text are mine. The published translations I adopted have been on occasion slightly modified.

Introduction to the English Edition

1.

In the summer of 1925, the visionary writer and inventor Hugo Gernsback, considered by some as one of the founders of "science fiction" (or "scientifiction," as he initially named it),[1] launched a bizarre invention, called *The Isolator*, designed to protect our minds against all possible distractions. The device was presented in the technology magazine *Science and Inventions* and advertised as follows:

> Most people who desire [...] to concentrate find it necessary to shut themselves up in an almost soundproof room in order to go ahead with their work, but even here there are many things that distract their attention.
>
> Suppose you are sitting in your study or your work room, ready for the task. Even if the window is shut, street noises filter through, and distract your attention. Someone slams a door in the house, and at once your trend of thought is disturbed.
>
> A telephone bell or a door bell rings somewhere, which is sufficient, in nearly all cases, to stop the flow of thought.
>
> But even if supreme quiet reigns, you are your own disturber practically fifty per cent of the time. You will lean back in your chair and begin to study the pattern of the wallpaper, or you will see a fly crawl along the wall, or a window curtain will be moving back and forth, all of which is often sufficient to turn your mind away from the immediate task to be performed.[2]

Numerous are the little things that can divert our attention when we are at work. The benefits of Gernsback's invention seem evident:

> The first helmet constructed as per illustration was made of wood, lined with cork inside and out, and finally covered with felt. There were three pieces of glass inserted for the eyes. In front of the mouth there is a baffle, which allows breathing but keeps out the sound [...].
>
> It will be noted that the glass windows directly in front of the eyes are black. The construction involved the use of ordinary window glass, the outer glass being painted entirely black. Two small white lines were scratched into the paint [...].
>
> The writer thought that shutting out the noises was not sufficient. The eye would still wander around, thereby distracting attention. By having the two white lines scratched on the glass, the field through which the eye can move is comparatively small [and] it is almost impossible to see anything except a sheet of paper in front of the wearer. There is, therefore, no optical distraction here.[3]

It is well known that Marcel Proust, obsessive writer and author of the seven-volume novel *À la recherche du temps perdu* (In Search of Lost Time), had cork panels lined against the walls of his room so as to protect his work and writing from outside noises.[4] But the setting presented here by Gernsback is even more extreme than Proust's cork prison. Since our own bodies, Gernsback argues, are more often than not a source of distraction, the isolator should first of all isolate us from ourselves. The best way to prevent distraction is to immobilize our body and eyes and limit any vital functions, including breathing, which is only allowed through a baffle in front of the mouth, later replaced by "a small oxygen tank," helping respiration while improving the soundproof quality of the helmet (Figure 1).

Gernsback concludes his article with an air of satisfaction and claims that, thanks to this arrangement, "an important task can be

The author at work in his private study aided by the Isolator. Outside noises being eliminated, the worker can concentrate with ease upon the subject at hand.

Figure 1 *The Isolator*, an invention by Hugo Gernsback (*Science and Invention*, vol. 13, no. 3, July 1925). Image courtesy of the Rare Book and Printed Materials Collection, Special Collections Research Center, Syracuse University Libraries.

completed in short order and the construction of the Isolator will be found to be a great investment." Unsurprisingly, however, his invention never caught on and it is likely that even Proust, plagued by asthma, would have found *The Isolator* quite impractical.

It is worth asking whether Gernsback's invention—at the borders between reality and science fiction—was intended to be slightly ironic in its uncompromising celebration of assiduous, efficient, and concentrated work. Regardless, if I have chosen to begin this book on distraction with a discussion of *The Isolator* it is because this invention perfectly conveys our common preconceptions and fears about distraction, which we usually see as a menace that literally besieges us on all sides, as a threatening enemy against which we must defend ourselves because it hinders the course of our thinking and jeopardizes our concentration and ability to work.

This book offers a different perspective, which goes hand in hand with a reevaluation and redefinition of distraction and its power, through readings and analyses of literary and philosophical texts. After all, as we will see, even in Proust's case, the need for distraction—for a creative distraction—proves to be an essential part of his life as well as of his work, to the point that even involuntary memory would be inconceivable without a willingness to be distracted by seemingly insignificant sensations.

But what is "distraction," exactly, and in what sense can we define it as a "power"?

2.

It is a commonplace that we live in the age of distraction, characterized by a crisis of attention. We hear every day that new technologies produce distraction,[5] that the powers that be want us to be distracted, unable to pay attention, and that the excess of stimuli to which we are exposed produces a deterioration of our "attentional resources."[6] But are we really sure that this is the case? One of the fundamental premises behind this book and its reevaluation of the "power of distraction" is that the problem today is not one of distraction but instead of the continuous and predetermined management of our attention, which prevents any distraction at all.[7] Rather than producing distraction, modern devices, on the contrary, are designed to exploit our attention. Distraction, understood in its proper sense, is profoundly alien and hostile to the techniques and mechanisms that monopolize our time and mental space.

Yves Citton and others have rightly spoken of the "economy of attention": "economy" not only in the sense of a monetization of our attention (from which earnings are made, if only in terms of "likes," "clicks," and "views"), but also in a more traditional sense of the "administration," "ordering," and "management" of our attention, which also implies the shaping of our perceptual environment (what has been called the "ecology of attention"). Not unlike Gernsback's surreal invention, today's new technological and digital devices seem increasingly to deprive us of the capacity for distraction, to separate us from the possibility of making free use of our attention. They tend to capitalize all our mental resources, to absorb and colonize, in the name of profit and productivity, all the empty moments in which a different and unmonitored form of attention could unfold. The verb "to attend," from Latin *attendere*, actually has more than one meaning, not necessarily mutually exclusive, from which we can deduce two types of attention: "to attend" denotes a "stretching towards," but also, in a more archaic sense, a state of waiting and passive expectation, a form of attentiveness without an object.[8]

The fact is, in a world where, as we say, "time is money," we feel that we don't have time to waste. We have the impression that abandoning ourselves to distraction or reverie is literally lost, if not stolen, time. So, as soon as we have some free or empty time—while we are sitting in a waiting room at the doctor's office or lining up at a ticket counter, during the suspended intervals of our daily errands—we rush into some short-term activity, which keeps us busy long enough to "kill time" and gives us the impression of "buying time" (checking emails or notifications, replying to a message, or looking at the latest news). Indeed, we greet with enthusiasm everything that allows us to "save time" while eliminating dead time.[9] Yet there lies a twofold paradox that cannot be ignored. On the one hand, the time thus gained is immediately spent on something else, so that a real gain is never obtained. On the other hand, it is precisely by trying to gain time that we actually lose it, or rather we lose that essential part of it which, as we will see in this book, can only come from moments of distraction. In order to grasp the sense of this paradox, we should reread Pascal, without however embracing his pessimistic views about human nature: our unhappiness derives not so much from being structurally incapable of remaining alone in a room and enduring boredom (according to Pascal's moralizing explanation that reproaches our human weakness or constitutive anthropological deficiency), but rather, I would argue, from having become unable to indulge in distraction.[10] Since we can be connected at any time, we can no longer be disconnected, as if the only time that is valid and worth living, because it produces objective and measurable results, is the time, paradoxically both shared and isolated simultaneously, that we spend online. We no longer have the time to be distracted by something unexpected and, despite the exponential growth of our cities, there are fewer and fewer *flâneurs* in our metropolises.

Although contemporary society is not my main focus, in this book I share Jonathan Crary's framework concerning the place of distraction and reverie today: our society is characterized not so much by distraction and mass deception as by an increasingly invasive seizure of attention, which excludes unproductive moments of daydream, any form of absent-minded introspection or unmonitored deviation of attention.[11] However, unlike Crary's bleak conclusions, this book would like to envisage a way out, by offering the tools for thinking and rediscovering distraction as a capacity that is at our disposal. More precisely, this book highlights the creative and subversive potential of moments of distraction, in which a free and idle form of attention can open up. The free use of attention is precisely what this book reclaims when speaking of the "power of distraction." "Power" here means precisely a *faculty* or *capacity* of the mind that we can reappropriate and learn to use in different ways.

3.

That distraction can be defined as a "power" in the sense of faculty or ability may seem counterintuitive. More than as a faculty, we usually think of distraction as the *absence* of a specific faculty (be it attention, thought, or intelligence). One of the fundamental theses at the core

Introduction to the English Edition 7

of this book is that distraction is by no means the negative or the opposite of attention. On the contrary, distraction is a different form of attention. This, however, could be understood in different ways. Being distracted often means paying attention to something else and, in a way, every act of attention implies a distraction: what we usually call distraction is simply the fact of paying attention to the *wrong thing*.[12] But, more importantly, distraction also involves a completely different form of attention: a form of attention that is not focal or mono-directional but diffuse, poly-vocal, and multidirectional. To the dominant idea of attention as a beam of light that we direct on certain objects and that can be occupied only by one thing at a time,[13] this book would like to add an idea of attention as diffuse receptivity, as the ability to pay attention, albeit in different degrees of clarity and confusion, to many different objects at the same time. Understood in these "Leibnizian" terms, attention becomes a function of memory and not of consciousness and will. This form of attention, which is actually at work in every moment, becomes more noticeable in states of distraction.

We often forget that a faculty is truly such (that is, a capacity that is freely available to us), when it maintains itself in relation to a "capacity not to." It is this possibility of doing and, at the same time, of not doing that opens a specific faculty to another possible use.[14] This means that attention is fully a faculty only when it is maintained in relation to the capacity for distraction, only when, by suspending the immediate relationship with an object that calls for our attention, we retain the ability to pay attention to something else, in other words to distract ourselves from what immediately attracts our attention.[15]

Writing about the interaction between human and machine, Simone Weil made an important distinction between *attention libre* (free attention) and *attention attachée* (attached or connected attention).[16] Unlike free attention, attached or connected attention absorbs and exhausts all our mental resources, preventing us from paying attention to anything else; it is, in this sense, the very opposite of distraction and reverie. Attached or connected attention causes the dialectic between attention and distraction (essential to *attention libre* and to a free exercise of attention as a power or faculty) to disappear. In its totalizing aspect, attached or connected attention is indissolubly tied to its object, from which it cannot turn away, not even for a moment.[17] While the latter is, for Simone Weil, the source of exploitation in a highly rationalized social and working environment, "free attention" is a pure power of attention, attention without a specific object and without immediate use. "Distraction" is a term that this book would like to reserve for all that is capable of freeing our attached or connected attention, making it available for other possible, non-predetermined uses.[18]

This is why the technological invasion of our mental space does not increase but rather reduces the possibilities for distraction. Suffice it to compare the ringing or beeping of a mobile phone to the buzzing of a fly (a distractive element par excellence in early modern philosophy and devotional literature, as well as in *The Isolator*). It is only apparently true that the ringing or beeping of a phone have a distracting power similar to that of the buzzing of a fly. The latter simply gives an unexpected detour to the course of our thoughts; it does not necessarily demand an answer. On the contrary, the beep of a telephone, even when it just informs us of a notification, calls us, identifies us because it is as if it were calling our name. It addresses us and demands an answer or, more precisely, a *reaction* (which can also be the simple act of turning off or silencing the phone). Unlike the buzz of a fly, the beep of a telephone coordinates our actions as simple reactions; on the contrary, the power of distraction is what separates us from a simple immediate reaction, opening up a series of possibilities that remain essentially indeterminate. In other words, the beep of a telephone does not release attached or connected attention making it available for other possible uses, but it is a simple capturing and monopolization of our attention that is snatched from one thing to be brought to another.

Of course, even the buzz of a fly can sometimes capture, monopolize, and immobilize our attention in an almost maniacal way, as in Le Clézio's "Assassinat d'une mouche,"[19] or in the "Fly" episode of *Breaking Bad* (third season, episode ten), entirely dedicated to catching an insect that inadvertently entered the laboratory. But this is not the only possible way of interacting with a distracting fly. In Proust's novel, it is in fact the buzzing of flies that becomes the musical background of the narrator's summer readings as a child. In Dreyer's film, *The Passion of Joan of Arc*, a fly that sneaks into the film set and lands on the face of the actress is creatively integrated as part of the scene, almost the materialization of the function of contingency within a work of art.[20] The flight of an insect can have the capacity to produce distraction, that is, to free our attention from the immediate present to make it available for other possible uses, which can also mean releasing its creative potential.

In its own way, that is also what this book sets out to do: explore and affirm the power of distraction.

4.

This book is organized in a thematic way around three of the main interrelated aspects or meanings of distraction: *divertissement*, "the power of flies," and *rêverie*. Each part explores one of these aspects, and what keeps the different parts together is not so much a logical progression as the presence of recurring themes, authors, and even characters or pseudo-characters (like La Bruyère's Ménalque). By returning to the question of distraction each time from different angles, these recurring motifs establish complicities, show resonances across works, and ultimately reflect on the significance of distraction as a power. This means that the book has several different points of entry, leaving it to the reader to decide where to begin.

Each part starts with an *avant-propos*, which is like a "focus" or point of convergence introducing, in a condensed form, the main idea to be developed. All its different threads, branches, and implications are then laid out in the subsequent sections, so that the book itself can be imagined as organized around a rhythmic alternation of moments of concentration and distraction.

Part One ("Divertissement") explores the moral-ethical aspect of distraction by looking at the notion of *divertissement*, its early meanings, and historical transformations. While for Montaigne *diversion* is essentially a positive life practice inspired by nature, in Pascal *divertissement* becomes a general tendency in our lives that reveals our wandering away from God, as a consequence of original sin. This shift from Montaigne's positive assessment of distraction to Pascal's condemnation of it is explained historically (via Pascal's reinterpretation of the question of diversion and *divertissement* within the context of Augustinian theology), but also analyzed theoretically, by turning to Gilles Deleuze's distinction between "ethics" and "morality" with regard to Spinoza. Although it is the Augustinian framework that, through Pascal, determines the dominant moral orientation through which we have continued to think distraction, the tension between these two possible assessments of distraction ("moral" and "ethical") continues to inhabit European thought during the Enlightenment and the Romantic period.

The title of Part Two ("The Power of Flies") is inspired by Pascal who, in his *Pensées*, revisits the motif of flies as a quintessential distractive element. This part explores the cognitive and creative aspect of the power of distraction in relation to contingency, the involuntary, and "signs," through the discussion of specific philosophical, scientific, and literary examples, from Augustine's conversion (narrated in Book VIII of the *Confessions*) to the illuminations of Poincaré and Proust, who both highlight the importance of distraction as a means of making unforeseen decisive discoveries or of remembering past memories that we seem to have forgotten. These examples are discussed in their differences and similarities in relation to other philosophical accounts, namely Kant's understanding of distraction as "mental hygiene," Pierre Cabanis's and Paul Chabaneix's description of the spontaneous mental processes determined by the mechanical awakening of ideas in dreams or states of distraction, and Freud's free-floating attention.

Part Three ("Rêverie") investigates the aesthetic-political dimension of the power of distraction. Following Locke, I show that reverie is not so much an absence of thinking as a different way of thinking or connecting ideas, close to dreaming and typical of childhood, which is displayed in moments of distraction. As such, reverie will be discussed in relation to fantasy, imagination, and hallucinations. Reverie implies the disarticulation of a given distribution of time and space as well as a material fusion with objects. Rousseau is among the first who defined reverie as an aesthetic experience whose political implications will be further explored, over the course of the eighteenth and nineteenth centuries, by authors such as Xavier de Maistre, Stendhal, or Baudelaire. Between the seventeenth and the nineteenth centuries, reverie and distraction were also associated with the phenomena of habit, automatism, and somnambulism. However, it is in relation to madness, with which they reveal a secret and almost forgotten affinity, that the social and political dimension of reverie and distraction can be fully grasped.

Building on some of the implications of Part Three, the Conclusion analyzes the complex relationship between laughter and distraction.

Each of these aspects of distraction is studied by adopting a non-systematizing approach, allowing definitions and conclusions to emerge from the different contexts in which ideas are tested. This essayistic method is inspired by my object of study, which essentially resists any systematic approach. In a way, I have attempted to practice, through my own writing, the very power or faculty that I am talking about, trying to unblock thoughts and ideas through distraction. In order to connect ideas and themes, to build meanings and interpretations, and to go from one subject to another, I have used a set of interconnected authors, texts, and cultural references from a modern and early modern French context. This is just one possible exploration of distraction, which does not exclude other possible investigations. The hope is, on the contrary, to be able to inspire more of them.

Oxford—Cingoli, August 2022

Introduction to the Italian Edition

1.

We have all experienced the unique power of distraction. We have spent hours thinking about a problem nagging at us; we have tried in vain to remember a name that was on the tip of our tongue. Often, the solution or name we have been looking for suddenly comes to our mind at the exact moment when we stop thinking about it and allow our attention to wander elsewhere. As it happens, this distraction or relaxation of the mind, commonly associated with guilt and considered a sign of laziness or lack of attention, proves to be a fundamental part of our psychic life, like a background noise that we should listen to from time to time.

From Augustine to Pascal and up to Heidegger, a dominant strain of Western thought has taught us to associate distraction either with sin and indolence or with dispersal and inauthenticity. Seen for centuries as one of the most noticeable symptoms of melancholy, distraction is still considered, by medical and psychiatric experts, to be an attention disorder requiring a specific type of treatment. Already in *The Anatomy of Melancholy*, Robert Burton describes melancholics as constantly distracted and intent on building castles in the air.[1] Even nowadays the "attention machine," an instrument that can display brain activity in real time and signal when the mind begins to wander, is considered a possible cure for depression.[2] Against the pitfalls and dangers of distraction, we have never stopped endorsing a form of thinking that promotes reflection and concentration, the rational control of desires, and the disciplining of passions.

This book tries to uncover a different philosophy of distraction, understood in the variety of its meanings and possible thematic variations—from *diversion* to *divertissement*, from involuntary memory to *rêverie*. This alternative philosophy takes shape through a constellation of themes and authors in which distraction is profiled as a particular way of seeing that can lead to a deeper understanding of reality, as a creative practice that can subvert the established order dividing the field of our attention. If, on the one hand, distraction is inevitable and the only way not to suffer its power is to accept it, on the other, it is a real capacity that we can learn to use and appropriate.

Going from Montaigne and Pascal to Bergson and Proust, and via authors such as La Bruyère, Voltaire, Rousseau, Xavier de Maistre, Leopardi, George Sand, or Baudelaire, this book attempts to refute commonplaces about distraction or to show their possible philosophical significance. Is it really true, for instance, that distraction implies a lack of attention and that when we are distracted we think of nothing at all? Is it not rather the case that, in moments of distraction, we are often able to grasp stimuli we are not normally aware of, to do tasks that seem to require great effort and application, or to remember people and situations that were apparently forgotten? And in what sense can one account, on a philosophical level, for the proverbial distraction of the artist or the scientist, accused of having their heads in the clouds? In some cases, distraction is only the other side of extreme concentration (in this sense, Théodule Ribot distinguished "dispersive distraction" from "absorbed distraction").[3] In other cases distraction proves to be a more elastic and dynamic form of attention, rooted in the senses, the imagination, and the body, and allowing the mind to test possibilities different or contrary to those it was intentionally focused on.

As literature and psychoanalysis show us, from Balzac to Freud, those who are distracted are almost always attentive to something else and see what eludes the attention of those who are too focused or concentrated. A tone of the voice, a rapid movement of the back, a characteristic in someone's gait, a slip in conversation can reveal something essential that escapes those who pay too much attention to what is being expressly said or done. It is precisely this capacity for distraction that characterizes the narrator's gaze in Proust's novel *À la recherche du temps perdu* (In Search of Lost Time). Just as a connoisseur recognizes the unmistakable hand of an artist by shifting attention from the main subjects of a painting to the most negligible and insignificant details, where the artist's conscious control is weaker, so a writer, analyst, or philosopher must be receptive to those impalpable yet telling details that lurk in the involuntary movements accompanying the voluntary ones, in the distracted gestures in which personal effort is less intense.

After all, without a certain disposition to be distracted, no one could enjoy reading a novel or watching a film, where excessive concentration prevents comprehension and makes it impossible to appreciate these activities. According to Henri Bergson, the purpose of art is precisely to produce distraction—an idea that can be understood in two ways. First of all, art produces distraction because, as we will see, it is able to radically transform our attention, so that we can see everyday things differently. Secondly, art has to do with distraction because, through a sort of hypnotic effect, it allows us to weaken the resistance of our self or personality, without which it would be impossible to feel the idea suggested by the artist and recreate it within ourselves.[4] This does not mean, however, that contemplation of works of art, being linked to distraction, should require a total loss of self or a suspension of thought.

Stendhal makes a particularly apt observation in this regard. For him, the pleasure of reading novels consists in nothing other than reverie: by resonating freely with what is occupying our minds at a given moment, a mental activity such as reading, like listening to a piece of music, would have the unique ability to absorb our attention without monopolizing it, allowing us, albeit indirectly and unintentionally, to think intensely about the object of our reveries. In other words, it is as if, while reading (but the same could be said for other forms of artistic experience, such as watching a film or a play), two parallel levels of thought are activated in the mind, two tracks on which different orders of ideas run. That is why, Stendhal notes, we can read the same novel over and over again across the years and find the same joy in it every time, albeit for different reasons.[5]

In much the same vein, Proust considered reading not only the noblest but also the most ennobling of all distractions because it allows us to get in touch with a different mind, to fully communicate with another way of thinking while continuing to develop our own, following ways and paths that we would have been incapable of finding without the impulse of what we are reading. This is why Proust saw in reading a form of communication which is fundamentally different from goal-oriented or polite conversation, since with conversation the moral and social obligations of courtesy and deference force us to eliminate moments of distraction and to replace silence with words, even when there is actually nothing to say.[6] Reading is an activity that, while keeping us occupied, does not take away space from reverie but rather favors it. On the contrary, frivolous conversation (unlike true friendships, where we communicate without condescension and we can remain silent without awkwardness) dominates our attention by focusing it on the present, making us feel obliged to fill all the sound gaps with words.[7]

These Proustian considerations are even more enlightening if we replace the worldly conversation Proust referred to with the situation created today by the different technological and digital devices that significantly enhance and increase all forms of communication.

The possibility of receiving emails, messages, and notifications of all kinds in real time, wherever we are, intensifies and speeds up communication, making our lives easier. At the same time, though, it determines a situation of *uninterrupted and ubiquitous conversation* that cuts down on pauses of silence and distraction, monopolizes our attention by channeling it into short-term occupations, and dictates the rapidity of our reactions and responses, which is increased to match the speed of communication. Gilles Deleuze once observed that we are indeed moving toward "control societies" which "operate through continuous control and instant communication."[8] However, thinking and creating, Deleuze also pointed out, have always been something different from communicating: "the key thing may be to create vacuoles of noncommunication, circuit breaks," gaps of silence, or moments of distraction and reverie, in which we might eventually find something new to say, something worth saying.[9]

2.

Even though an analysis of contemporary society is far from being the focus of this book, it will not be difficult to see, in many of the themes it covers, possible links with the present age, marked by the digital revolution and technological invasion, due to which distraction seems to have become an integral part of our ordinary experience. We tend to think of distraction as a phenomenon that has intensified with technological development. From every side of the political spectrum, we are told that today we live in the "age of distraction." It is worth asking, however, whether these devices really do produce distraction, as is usually said, or whether they are, on the contrary, ways of capturing and saturating our attention. As we will see, distraction is in itself a much more ancient and philosophically complex phenomenon than it appears in everyday language, where this term often has only a *relative* meaning and indicates nothing other than a *distraction from* (in this sense, every form of attention is a distraction from something else and vice versa). When we say that mobile phones or social media are a cause of distraction we only scratch the surface and leave the true power of distraction unthought. On closer examination, the effect of such devices is not so much distraction as it is defined and reclaimed in this book but the *continuous and programmed management of our attention.*

Starting with the analyses of Gabriel Tarde in the late nineteenth century, it has become clear how technology and mass media are not so much "weapons of mass distraction" (according to a much-abused empty slogan) as, on the contrary, as Yves Citton rightly reminds us, "collective attentional devices."[10] As such, they are aimed at concentrating, organizing, and now even recording our attention, so as to ensure the perpetuation of specific perceptual, interpretative, and behavioral patterns that only a truly distracted gaze is able to break, thanks to its ability to create unpredictable deviations and bifurcations.[11] Rather than producing distraction, these technologies seem to provide us with pre-packaged ways of occupying our time, saturating all the mental space that is free from work or other daily activities. It is not a question here of accusing technology and condemning it unreservedly, but of pointing out that, despite what we may superficially believe, the problem today is not so much distraction but its opposite—that is, an excess of attention which leaves the mind less and less time (and less and less space) to wander or drift along unpredictable lines of flight.

3.

It was once pointed out to me that Pascal, like most authors discussed here, has been dead for quite some time now: why dwell so much on him in a book that talks about distraction *today*? Put another way, why resort to the philosophy and literature of past eras to deal with such a current and urgent problem? There are other branches of knowledge (from psychology and cognitive science to sociology) which would seem to be better equipped to provide answers and analyses that are much more up-to-date and in line with the times. When this objection was addressed to me, in the somewhat alienating context of a job interview, I did not have a convincing answer ready—meaning an answer that was not rhetorical, abstract, or self-referential (the vital role that certain authors have played in our tradition and without which we could not possibly understand … etc. etc.). But, as often happens, in keeping with what the French call *l'esprit de l'escalier* (staircase wit)—which is also, if you like, a perfect example of the power of distraction—the right answer only came to me later. Indeed, the right answer always comes to mind later, once we stop thinking about it and we are already at the bottom of the staircase, so to speak, on our way out and have already finished writing.

Oxford, June 2020

Part One

Divertissement

Avant-propos

Whenever we have to make an important decision and we look for any excuse to procrastinate, whenever we have to face a vexing problem and we take every opportunity to think of something else, we fall prey to the mechanism that Pascal described as *divertissement*. In Pascal's philosophical lexicon, *divertissement* indicates the mostly unconscious dynamic through which people turn their eyes away from the fundamental questions or tasks of their existence and approach death without realizing it. That is why *divertissement*, "the only thing which consoles us for our miseries," is in fact for Pascal "the greatest of our miseries": it makes us look like fools who fearlessly run along the edge of a precipice after covering our eyes so as not to see it.[1]

Unlike the English term "amusement" (often used to translate the French *divertissement*), Pascal's *divertissement* includes not only entertainment, amusements, and leisure activities, but also all those commitments, daily tasks, business, and chores of all kinds that fill our days and distract us from thinking seriously about ourselves. A more accurate translation of Pascal's *divertissement* would be "diversion" or "distraction." In the words of another philosopher chronologically closer to us, Martin Heidegger, *divertissement* could be defined as that way of existing in which human beings live inauthentically (*uneigentlich*), far from themselves, completely captivated by the banality of everyday life, and dragged along by an anxious industriousness that prevents them from accessing their most authentic existential possibilities.[2]

It is often the case that when we are dealing with an important issue that requires calm and concentration, we become more prone to distraction. We need to stop and think, to put our thoughts in order, but instead we keep scrolling through our Facebook Newsfeed, which, like a wishing well, has the advantage of being bottomless, or we run around frantically in all directions, prey to a frenzy of activity that completely absorbs us. Indeed, it is not uncommon for this kind of hyperactivity to be the symptomatic counterpart of some preoccupation which we try to escape by focusing outwards, but which invariably returns as soon as we are left alone with ourselves, with nothing to distract us. It is then that boredom (*ennui*) takes possession of our soul:

> Nothing is so intolerable to man as to be completely at rest, without passions, without business, without diversion [*divertissement*], without effort [*application*]. Then he feels his nothingness, his abandonment, his inadequacy, his dependence, his weakness, his emptiness. At once from the depths of his souls arises boredom, gloom, sadness, fretfulness, vexation, despair.
>
> (*Pensées*, 515)

Judging by the procession of passions that accompany it (gloom, sadness, fretfulness, vexation, and despair), and which recall medieval acedia or melancholy,[3] the *ennui* described by Pascal does not seem to have much in common with the state of mind designated under the same name by modern literature and psychology, where this term indicates the disgust, malaise, or languor that arises from monotony or lack of activity. This is the definition we find for instance in Diderot and d'Alembert's *Encyclopédie*[4] and which is implicit in current language when we say, for example, that we are bored or that something is boring us. Understanding the term *ennui* in a sense closer to the modern one, Pierre Nicole, one of Pascal's colleagues at Port-Royal, accused him of confusing "boredom" and "sadness." In a letter to Renaud de Sévigné (the uncle of Madame de Sévigné and stepfather of Madame de La Fayette) Pierre Nicole argued that boredom never arises from a particular thought, however painful and unpleasant it may be, but rather from a *lack* of thought, from a cessation of the mind's activity: this is why the feeling described by Pascal, which pervades us when we think of something that afflicts us (be it death, the misery of the human condition, or the nothingness of all things) is not boredom but sadness. Furthermore, criticizing Pascal even more harshly and without hiding his vexation at Madame de La Fayette's appreciation of him, in the same latter Pierre Nicole insisted that sadness does not drive us to seek out leisure and occupation, but to avoid them.[5]

What does Pascal mean by *ennui* if, like sadness, it arises from thought (and not from an absence of thought) and yet, unlike sadness, *ennui* generates restlessness, a need for distraction and a wish to escape from the self? In Pascal's work, *ennui* seems to have the same depth as the existential and metaphysical "anxiety" (*Angst*) analyzed by Heidegger in *Being and Time* and *What Is Metaphysics?* Even more so than the "profound boredom" (*tiefe Langweile*) studied in *Fundamental Concepts of Metaphysics*, it is "anxiety" that appears to reflect some of the essential features of Pascal's ennui. Profound boredom, according to Heidegger, is not despairing but *revealing*, and forces us to listen to our most authentic being.[6] Instead, anxiety, often mistakenly confused with "fear" (*Furcht*), contains two opposite possibilities: it can bring about either a *conversion*, an opening toward the authentic, or a *diversion*, a turning back from it (such as when, in the indefinite malaise of anxiety, we try to fill the void of silence with nonsense and "idle talk").[7] This double possibility is also contained in Pascal's *ennui*, which on the one hand nourishes the need for distraction and escape in *divertissement*, and on the other hand represents something that, if we were able to listen to it, would prompt us to find a more solid way out—that is, turning to God.

1. Montaigne and Pascal, or the Difference between Ethics and Morality

Pascal uses the term "divertissement" in a strictly etymological sense (from the Latin *divertere*, to turn elsewhere, in the opposite direction), according to a meaning that had already fallen into disuse in the seventeenth century, when *divertissement* began to be used as the equivalent of amusement. Pascal derives this archaism from Montaigne, more precisely from chapter 4 of the third book of *Les Essais* entitled "De la diversion" ("On Diversion"), where *divertissement* (also a synonym of *fourvoiement*, misdirection) is primarily a stratagem that consists in diverting someone or something.[1]

According to Montaigne, this technique can be applied to the most varied objects, such as phlegm, army troops, passions, desires, and thoughts, and can find its employment in a wide variety of fields—from military maneuvers to medicine and the treatment of suffering in the soul, such as melancholy, mourning, or heartache. Montaigne, however, concentrates on what we would call today the "psychological" use of this technique, describing a veritable strategy, or rather a *tactic*[2] of distraction applicable both to others and to ourselves:

> [S]ome painful idea gets hold of me; I find it quicker to change it than to subdue it. If I cannot substitute an opposite one for it, I can at least find a different one. Change always solaces it, dissolves it, and dispels it. If I cannot fight it, I flee it; and by my flight I made a diversion and use craft; by changing place, occupation, and company I escape from it into the crowd of other pastimes and cogitations, in which it loses all track of me and cannot find me.[3]

If this practice, as Montaigne recognizes, could remind us of Epicurus's suggestion to shift one's thoughts from the troublesome to the pleasant in order to overcome sadness, however, Montaigne adds a further aspect to it, borrowed from nature itself. Thanks to time, "the sovereign doctor of our griefs" (*Essais*, III, ch. 4, Fr. 836, Eng. 941), nature manages to dissolve and gradually to corrode even the most painful feelings, providing new objects and occupations for our imagination. Likewise, diversion must be gentle and gradual, administered little by little, so as to free us *imperceptibly* from the thought that is grieving us. Wishing *not* to think about something means already thinking about it; that is why we are not successful when we seek to resist painful thoughts head-on: "for opposition spurs them on and involves them more deeply in sadness; the grief is aggravated by anger at the contention" (*Essais*, III, ch. 4, Fr. 830, Eng. 935).

For Montaigne, resorting to the tactic of diversion means nothing other than encouraging the natural tendency toward change and transformation inherent in all things. Diversion is not only beneficial to us, but it is also part of life itself and intervenes in our thought processes at all times, even without us being aware of it: "our thoughts are always elsewhere: the hope of a better life arrests us and comforts us" (*Essais*, III, ch. 4, Fr. 834, Eng. 939). After all, how can we not be distracted when everything around us (even the Earth, the rocks of the Caucasus, and the pyramids of Egypt) is constantly changing, minute after minute, and constancy itself is nothing but slow movement? (*Essais*, III, ch. 2, Fr. 804–5, Eng. 907–8).

Here, despite the etymological proximity, we see an obvious gap between Pascal's *divertissement* and the *diversion* theorized by Montaigne. This gap is a matter not only of assessment (distraction has a positive function in Montaigne and a negative one in Pascal) but also of structure: while for the author of *Les Essais*, *diversion* is essentially a life practice inspired by nature, in Pascal *divertissement* becomes a general tendency of human life in the condition of sin. Unlike *diversion*, *divertissement* involves a person's entire existential conduct and is characterized as a fall from God to the world, from truth to falsehood, from reality to appearance, from what is stable and eternal to what is changeable and perishable.[4]

Pascal draws this understanding of the value and function of distraction from Augustine. He reinterprets the whole question of *diversion* and *divertissement* against the background of Augustinian theology and, more specifically, the *aversio/conversio* dyad. The movement of distraction from God toward creatures (*aversio a Deo* and *conversio ad creaturam*), which for Augustine was a consequence of original sin and contained in turn the essence of all sins, is precisely what Pascal revisits and modernizes through the notion of *divertissement*, giving it an existential rather than a theological connotation.[5] It is thus the Augustinian source, rather than the background originally provided by Montaigne, that profoundly shaped Pascal's notion of *divertissement* and bequeathed it to Western thought, thereby determining the moral orientation through which we continue to think about the phenomenon of distraction.

The difference in attitude between Montaigne and Pascal when it comes to distraction can perhaps be clarified by resorting to Deleuze's distinction between "ethics" and "morality" with regard to Spinoza. According to this distinction, while morality is based on transcendent values and absolute oppositions, such as good and evil, ethics involves the simple immanent consideration of what, case by case, proves to be "good" or "bad" for life itself (an encounter, a practice, an idea). This is why, as Deleuze points out quoting Nietzsche, even for Spinoza "beyond Good and Evil at least this *does not* mean: beyond good and bad."[6] If "good" is what is in accord with our nature and strengthens our vital power, "bad" is what on the contrary diminishes it and diverges from it. The most eloquent example is for Spinoza that of a poison that breaks down blood: the poison is not evil in itself, although it is bad for us because, operating according to its nature, it forms relations of composition with our body that no longer correspond to our essence.[7]

Going back to Pascal and Montaigne, we could argue that for Pascal distraction is essentially a "moral" problem—that is, a problem which is examined based on the absolute opposition between God and the world, between true and false, and between reality and appearance. Instead, for Montaigne distraction is a matter to be considered solely from an "ethical" point of view, regardless of absolute or transcendent values, but based on the simple immanent consideration of what is good or bad for us and for our lives case by case, of what increases or decreases our happiness and vital power in specific circumstances.

This is why Pascal emphasizes *divertissement* as a state, as a condition of dispersion and decadence determined by sin and thus inscribed in the sphere of an original fault that we renew every day by indulging in distraction. Instead, Montaigne focuses on *diversion* as a practice for good and healthy living, diametrically opposed to repentance, which implies a useless fixation on painful thought. In chapter 2 of the third book *Les Essais* entitled "Du repentir" ("On Repentance"), Montaigne admits that he rarely repents: "my conscience is happy with itself, not as the conscience of an angel or a horse, but as the conscience of a man" (*Essais*, III, ch. 2, Fr. 806, Eng. 909). His conscience is happy with itself not because it is sure of its own infallibility, firmness, and stability (only an angel could boast of this), but because it is aware of the mutability and fickleness of human nature. Furthermore, Montaigne continues, "my actions are ruled by what I am and are in harmony with my condition of life. I cannot do better: and the act of repenting does not properly concern things that are not in our power" (*Essais*, III, ch. 2, Fr. 813, Eng. 916). This implies, first, that there is no point in repenting what we have done (even if we can feel sorry about it) because we can only ever act in conformity with what we are. Second, just as we cannot regret not being what we are not (say, angels or horses) because this is not within our power, there is no reason to regret being fragile, changeable, and contradictory creatures, naturally prone to and in need of distraction. While recognizing, not unlike Pascal, the weakness and frivolity of human nature ("we can be distracted and diverted by small things, since small things are capable of holding us", *Essais*, III, ch. 4, Fr. 836, Eng. 942), Montaigne, however, is careful not to view this as an imperfection to be corrected or the result of a fault requiring atonement.

As in Spinoza, so in Montaigne can we also find what Deleuze called a "philosophy of life"[8]—a philosophy whose aim is to expose and avoid everything that separates us from life, including all the values that are directed against it. As Montaigne observes, "what makes for human happiness is not, as Antisthenes said, dying happily but living happily" (*Essais*, III, ch. 2, Fr. 816, Eng. 920).[9] In a hypothetical philosophical dialogue between the dead, of the kind imagined by Fontenelle, the author of *Les Essais* might have replied likewise to Pascal, who accused him of inspiring "indifference about salvation, without fear and without repentance" (*Pensées*, 559).

2. The "Sublime Misanthropist": Voltaire against Pascal

Voltaire is credited with one of the most penetrating critiques of Pascal's conception of *divertissement*. In his "petit Anti-Pascal"[1]— the twenty-fifth of the *Lettres philosophiques* (Philosophical Letters), first published in English and then printed in France in 1734 with the addition of the last letter—Voltaire described the author of the *Pensées* as a "sublime misanthropist," an enemy of all humanity, who portrayed humankind as inherently evil and unhappy, condemned in its entirety to sin and error.[2] The problem of *divertissement* proved to be one of the testing grounds for a series of theological and anthropological questions that prompted Voltaire to engage in polemical confrontations with Pascal throughout his life.[3]

For Voltaire, it is not a question of merely countering Pascal's condemnation of distraction with the exaltation of worldly pleasures, according to a simplistic hedonism that flattens the difference between *divertissement* and amusement. Voltaire's strategy is more complex and involves two moves. Firstly, he shows how human activity, which Pascal rejects entirely as a mere form of distraction, is an integral part of the perfect realization of our nature: "Man is born for action as sparks fly upward and a stone drops. Not to be active and not to exist are the same thing for humankind. The sole difference is in the activity, gentle or tumultuous, dangerous or useful."[4] Here too the point is to adopt an ethical (and not a moral) criterion to assess what favors or hinders the expression and realization of our nature.

Playing billiards or royal tennis, writing philosophy books or composing verse, dedicating oneself to the search for truth or chasing a hare, going to war or to the theater, gambling, dancing, singing, chatting, sailing, or holding prestigious posts: all these activities, the list of which could be continued at will, are for Pascal on exactly the same level. They are different but equivalent ways of occupying time in order to distract oneself from the most important things, first and foremost thinking about death: "Without examining every particular pursuit, it is enough to comprehend them under diversion [*divertissement*]" (*Pensées*, 713). Being no more than a form of distraction, hunting is no less valuable than poetry, and there is nothing wrong in preferring the former to the latter, as indeed most people do. It is only the "half-learned," who do not fully understand human misery, that scoff at ordinary occupations and think they express the "world's foolishness" (*Pensées*, 134). Even philosophy, Pascal points out, is just an occupation like any other: Plato and Aristotle themselves, like everyone else in need of distraction, wrote their works simply to occupy their time, and this was the least philosophical part of their lives. What Pascal condemns under the name of *divertissement* is thus human life as a whole. Work, travel, study, love, friendship, pleasures, interests of all kinds: all this is nothing but vanity because it drags us away from ourselves in a continuous flight from the present and from truth.

In a close battle with selected passages from the *Pensées*, Voltaire endeavors to overturn the value system underlying Pascal's critique of *divertissement*: a value system, as we have seen, of Augustinian origin, which clearly opposes love of God and love of any created thing, erasing all intermediate nuances within the spectrum between these two incompatible poles. For Voltaire, not only are these two types of love compatible with one another (it is indeed our duty to love created things), but the very realization of human happiness, as intended by God, requires us to enjoy fully the goods that are available to us in the world (*Lettres philosophiques*, Letter 25, X). It is a question neither of viewing the universe as a prison where people live awaiting execution (according to an image used by Pascal) nor of seeing the world as a place of delights intended solely for the pleasure of the senses (this would be the dream of a hedonist). Rather, humans and animals are simply what they must be according to their nature. The large metropolises that boomed at the beginning of the eighteenth century and their elegant luxuries praised in the poem "Le Mondain"[5] are for Voltaire an evidence of how people naturally seek pleasure. Pascal compared his dismay at the human condition on Earth to the despair of someone who, carried off to a desert island while sleeping, wakes up in the morning not knowing where they are or whether there is some way to escape. To such remarks, Voltaire replied ironically: "As for me, when I look at Paris or London, I see no reason whatever to feel the despair that M. Pascal describes. I see a city that does not in the least resemble a desert island but is inhabited, opulent, well ordered, where men are as happy as human nature permits" (*Lettres philosophiques*, Letter 25, VI).

Pascal blamed the fickleness of human nature and the ease with which pursuing a ball or a hare can relieve us of the deepest pain, such as the death of a loved one. Echoing Montaigne, Voltaire comments on the severity of this remark arguing that nature itself has given us diversion and dissipation as remedies for suffering (*Lettres philosophiques*, Letter 25, XXVII). It is indeed significant that a similar example is reused by Voltaire in his definition of *frivolité* (frivolity), a mental disposition that closely resembles diversion and without which life would simply be intolerable:

> We are sometimes ruminant oxen crushed under the yoke, sometimes scattered doves that flee trembling from the vulture's claw, disgusted by the blood of our companions; foxes chased by dogs; tigers that devour each other. Suddenly we become butterflies, and as we flutter we forget all the horrors we have experienced.[6]

But the positive function of distraction is not limited to the fact that it frees us from anguish, projects us toward the future, and grounds both our happiness and any form of sociality. More simply (this is Voltaire's second and more radical move) we could not live without relating to the outside world, without abandoning ourselves to outside stimuli. Without a relationship with the outside world there would be no life, just as there would be no thought. Ideas, like the food we eat and the air we breathe, come from outside, from the senses and from experience (*Lettres philosophiques*, Letter 25, XXXIV and XXXVII). For Voltaire, rejecting Pascal's condemnation of *divertissement* is not simply a matter of promoting human activity in its proper sphere or of celebrating distraction as a strategy to avoid thinking about our miseries. For Voltaire, it is instead a matter of going deeper and reexamining the whole question of *divertissement* by replacing the austere theological anthropology embraced by the author of the *Pensées*, centered on the idea of original sin, with an anthropology that builds on the premises established by Locke's philosophy, already enthusiastically presented in the thirteenth of the *Lettres philosophiques*.[7]

It is the adoption of this philosophical perspective (even more than his Jesuit upbringing) that allows Voltaire to "naturalize" distraction, questioning the clear opposition, presupposed by Pascal, between inside and outside, between inward and outward. Our relationship with the outside is simply inescapable, and the need for distraction itself is neither a consequence of the Fall nor a way of distracting ourselves from thinking about our condition. Rather, it has an incontrovertible anthropological foundation, linked to the simple fact that we have a body and that our mental life is necessarily mediated by the senses. Human beings are not the enigma or unfathomable mystery that Pascal would have us believe when he portrays us as contradictory beings, split between God and the world, between interiority and exteriority, suspended between greatness and misery. Our unpredictable behavior and tendency toward distraction are simply the result of the quantity of objects, cases, and circumstances that condition our behavior on a daily basis.

This is why one of the central points of Voltaire's refutation of Pascal in the twenty-fifth letter consists in questioning the image—or rather the proof—on which the author of the *Pensées* based his entire discourse on human misery: that of a man left alone in a room, with nothing to distract him, who is forced to think solely of himself. In reality, Voltaire retorts, even in the solitude of a room, the place of interior recollection par excellence, man cannot help but live and think outside himself.

3. One Man Alone in a Room

It would be a mistake to say that Pascal promotes a simple return to the self and to inwardness. As we read in one of the *Pensées*, "Self is hateful," unbearable, because "it makes itself the center of everything" and is the source of all injustice and disorder. If it is true that the supreme good to which we aspire is found inward rather than outward, nevertheless inner self-sufficiency is an unattainable ideal because it does not take into account the fickleness of human nature. And, to tell the truth, the happiness we seek—Pascal points out, recovering an Augustinian type of logic—"is neither outside us nor within us" because it is found in God, who is "both outside and within us" and belongs to all without being anyone's exclusive property (*Pensées*, 26). If we have to look inward it is only to find the drive toward something that transcends us. If *divertissement* is bad, and indeed is the worst of our miseries, it is because, by distracting us from the task of thinking about ourselves, it also prevents us from thinking about God, on whom our salvation depends and toward whom we would turn if we were aware of our situation. *Divertissement* is therefore condemned by Pascal not so much as a distraction from oneself as a *distraction from God*—from a more authentic possibility of life, which we would achieve by returning to ourselves.

The Stoics, Pascal argues, placed happiness in the tranquility of self-sufficiency and invited us to withdraw into our inner selves and resist temptations coming from the outside; human beings, on the other hand, instinctively embrace a different view when they abandon themselves to the distractions offered by the external world. While rejecting both positions, Pascal finds himself much closer to the latter. In fact, this perspective is at least aware of human weakness and admits that we cannot find happiness alone. On the contrary, Pascal claims, philosophers who simply urge us to withdraw into ourselves and renounce the world show an underestimation of the amount of things we are distracted by every day, which draw us out of ourselves through the lure of the senses and the passions (*Pensées*, 240).

The fact remains, however, that Pascal's discourse on *divertissement* is underpinned by the opposition between an inside and an outside, between an interiority (a private place of quietude, recollection, and introspection) and an exteriority (where dispersion and escape unfold, dragging us both outside ourselves and away from God). This spatial opposition is reinforced by the well-known example of a man left alone in a room, from which Pascal deduces all the reasons for human unhappiness:

> On the occasions when I have pondered over men's various activities, the dangers and worries they are exposed at Court or at war, from which so many quarrels, passions, risky, often ill-conceived actions and so on are born, I have often said that man's unhappiness springs from one thing alone, his incapacity to stay quietly in one room. If a man had enough to live on and if he knew how to stay happily at home, then he would not leave to go to sea, or besiege a town. You only buy a commission in the army, which is so expensive, if you cannot bear being unable to leave town. You only go out of your way to find conversation or card games [*les conversations et les divertissements*], if you cannot remain happily at home. Etc.
>
> But when I thought more closely about it, and, having found the cause of all our unhappiness, wanted to discover the reason, I found that there was a truly powerful one which lies in the natural unhappiness of our feeble, mortal condition, so wretched that nothing can console us when we think about it.
>
> Whatever position we imagine with all the conceivable wealth of which we can conceive for ourselves, royalty is the best station in the world. However, let us consider that position with every possible satisfaction which can go with it. If a king has no distraction [*divertissement*] and is allowed to consider and reflect on what he is, that fragile happiness will not sustain him. He will inevitably fall into thinking about situations which threaten him with rebellions, and finally about death and illness which are inevitable. So, if he has nothing in the way of so-called distractions [*s'il est sans divertissement*], he will be unhappy, unhappier even than the humblest of his subjects who can play games and enjoy themselves.
>
> That is why gaming and the conversation of women, war, and great offices of the state are so sought after [...].

That is why we like noise and activity so much. That is why imprisonment is such a horrific punishment. That is why the pleasure of being alone is incomprehensible.

(*Pensées*, 168)

After the image of the "thinking reed," this is probably Pascal's best-known and most-repeated motif. First taken up by La Bruyère ("All men's misfortunes proceed from their aversion to being alone; hence gambling, extravagances, dissipation, wine, women, ignorance, slander, envy, and forgetfulness of what we owe to God and ourselves"),[1] this theme would also return, as we shall see, in Maine de Biran and Baudelaire.

Left alone in a room, with nothing preventing us from becoming aware of the truth from which we usually prefer to divert our eyes, we would realize that our external happiness is only apparent and temporary, potentially threatened by chance and countless accidents and misfortunes that can occur at any time and against which there is no possible guarantee. In the solitude of a room, even a king, apparently the happiest and most comfortable of men, becomes more unhappy than the least of his subjects. The need for distraction levels people, without distinction of rank or fortune. Not only does it equate kings and subjects, the learned and the ignorant, the healthy and the sick (*Pensées*, 181),[2] but it also reverses hierarchies. The more powerful and wealthy a person is, the more they will be overcome by worry if left to themselves, crushed by the weight of their responsibilities, and therefore in need of distraction. The same idea is repeated in another fragment: "The great and the humble have the same misfortunes, the same griefs, the same passions; but the one is at the top of the wheel, and the other near the center, and so less disturbed by the same revolutions" (*Pensées*, 593). Voltaire will not fail to see the paternalistic snobbery entailed by this comparison, which he considers to be as ingenious as it is false, because in reality a poor man without resources, left alone thinking, will certainly have more problems to contend with than someone who at least has the necessary wealth to mitigate the possible blows of fate (*Lettres philosophiques*, Letter 25, XXXVIII). But this is not the real point of Voltaire's criticism.

In writing his *Pensées*, Pascal had decided to set aside his training as a mathematician and physicist so as to adopt an "order" of exposition that differed from the demonstrative style of geometry and the exact sciences. This method, employed in particular by Descartes, appeared to him to be less effective in matters of religion and morality than the more vague and digressive style of Montaigne.[3] However, his scientific training shines through, if not in the approach and method adopted, then in the "experimental" character of the hypothetical situations that are set up for us as tests or thought experiments. Just as the scientist artificially recreates in the laboratory the ideal conditions for the study of a given phenomenon, so Pascal asks the reader to imagine fictitious situations in order to isolate a characteristic of the human condition he wishes to observe.[4] This procedure is particularly evident in the analysis of *divertissement*: "Let us try it out. If a king is left entirely alone, with no means of satisfying his senses, nothing to worry about, no company and only himself to think about, you will see that a king without distraction [*divertissement*] is a man full of wretchedness" (*Pensées*, 169).

One of the aspects contested by Voltaire is precisely the adoption of this argumentative strategy, which consists in hypothetically positing extreme conditions, far removed from ordinary life and constructed by adding or subtracting certain variables at will, in order to infer general and definitive conclusions about human nature. In Voltaire's eyes, such a procedure, vaguely reminiscent of the scientific method, cannot but be fallacious and deceptive from a moral and anthropological point of view because it implies necessary and deliberate simplifications.[5] Let us take the example of a man left alone in a room, thinking only of himself. Given such a situation, says Voltaire, there are only two possibilities: either this man will be reduced to a larval state and will think of nothing at all, or he will necessarily think of something that comes to him from outside.

> This phrase "consider only ourselves" means nothing. What could a man be who does not act, and who is presumed to contemplate himself? Not only do I say that such a man is an imbecile, useless to society, but also that such a man could not exist; for what would such a man contemplate, his body, his feet, his hands, his five senses? Either he would be an idiot or else he would be using all these things. Would he simply contemplate his ability to think? But he cannot contemplate this ability without using it. Either he will think of nothing, or he will think of ideas that he has already had, or he will invent new ones; now, he can only have ideas that come from outside him. Thus he is necessarily preoccupied either by his senses or by his ideas.
>
> (*Lettres philosophiques*, Letter 25, XXIII)

The expression particularly contested by Voltaire ("consider only ourselves") was actually added by the first editors of the *Pensées*, published posthumously in 1670, in the so-called Port-Royal edition. This, however, does not change the substance of his critique, whose fundamental point remains the following: it is simply impossible for human beings *to think only of themselves*—that is, to withdraw the mind from its essential and constitutive relationship with the external world, mediated by the senses and the body. As Locke himself showed, ideas come from outside: if our senses were not oriented toward our surroundings, if we were impervious to the influence of the outside world, we would be devoid of thought and ideas. We live and think outside ourselves even when we are alone in a room.

The truly decisive aspect of Voltaire's critique consists in undermining any rhetoric of introspection, the same rhetoric that still today underlies the condemnation of distraction, often accused of making us lose contact with our inner life or our most authentic and inmost selves. For Voltaire, it is not simply a matter of rejecting introspection because thinking about oneself is painful and it is therefore legitimate to try in every way to escape this torment. In doing so, even if one were to overturn Pascal's value system, one would still be trapped in his logic, as indeed happens to the libertine Saint-Évremond.[6] The objection raised by Voltaire is even more radical and consists in affirming that there is no interiority as such.[7]

After all, there is a fact that Montaigne had not failed to notice when he decided to retire into solitude to devote himself to complete idleness (*Essais*, I, ch. 8) and that Xavier de Maistre perfectly staged in his subtle parody of Pascal called *Voyage autour de ma chamber* (Voyage around My Room): the mind finds infinite ways of digressing and entertaining itself even—or rather, perhaps even more so—in solitude. This is why, when in *Spleen de Paris*, quoting Pascal and La Bruyère, Baudelaire apparently revisited this Pascalian motif, according to which all human unhappiness derives from the inability to be alone in a room, he said something rather different from Pascal. To a "philanthropic journalist," fervently convinced that "solitude is bad for humankind," the poet replies that this is definitely true of the "chatterbox": "Certainly a chatterbox, whose supreme pleasure is to spout from a pulpit or rostrum, if put on Robinson Crusoe's island is not at all unlikely to go raving mad."[8] Indeed, solitude provides a kind of pleasure that is completely unknown to egocentrics of this kind, whose greatest satisfaction consists in always being the center of attention. Furthermore, as we will see in Part Three, this is a pleasure that those truly enamored of solitude can also find in a busy crowd: "Multitude, solitude: equal and convertible terms for the active and productive poet."[9]

4. Maine de Biran Criticizing (Voltaire Criticizing) Pascal

Voltaire's objections to Pascal were bound to seem inaccurate to many later readers. Pascal does not always seem to be saying what Voltaire claims he is, by artfully extrapolating specific statements from their context. For example, when Pascal writes that a man alone in a room is forced to think only of himself, a more cautious interpreter would surely observe that Voltaire takes this expression too literally.[1] Pascal does not claim that an individual in this situation completely loses sight of the outside world in order to contemplate only his own self but merely observes that, in the solitude of a room, without occupations to distract him, even the man least inclined to reflection will suddenly be forced to become aware of a truth he usually prefers not to think about.

However, this does not invalidate Voltaire's critique, which aims to highlight another side of the problem. To say that there is no interiority separate from an exteriority—that humans cannot help thinking at all times about what is outside themselves—is to argue a very simple thing, namely that at no time is our mental life completely protected from the interference of external factors of which we are only partly aware. Nothing, not even absolute isolation, can preserve us from this external influence. Like all other animals, in fact, humans depend entirely on the environment in which they live: their bodies are in a constant osmotic relationship with their surroundings and this conditions their mental life at all times. The climate, atmospheric changes, the air we breathe, and the food we eat are always affecting the way we think, feel, and desire. The alteration of an organ is enough to modify our intellect or our will (*Lettres philosophiques*, Letter 25, III and IV). If this is the case, how can we be sure that the reflections of a man in the solitude of a room are the authentic manifestation of some supposed inner truth and not, say, the expression of a bad disposition produced by a lack of light or fresh air, excessive cold or heat, or by a lack of movement?

It is for this reason that, at the beginning of the following century, Voltaire's objections could not be ignored by a reader like Maine de Biran—the philosopher who perhaps more than anyone else sensed the mutability of our inner being, dominated by countless external factors, and throughout his life strove to find some way to give stability to the self. To be sure, Maine de Biran did not fail to attack Voltaire. His error, in Biran's view, consisted in arguing that, since ideas come from outside, then to think about these ideas is equivalent to being outside oneself. Furthermore, according to Maine de Biran, Voltaire (like all modern philosophers who follow sensationism) did not take into account the experience of the inner sense, which shows that the activity of the thinking principle does not necessarily require a relationship with the outside but can be exercised in itself.[2] Nevertheless, while formally defending Pascal against accusations that he deemed vulgar and superficial, Maine de Biran could not entirely dismiss Voltaire's criticism, which he took far more seriously than he admitted.

In 1815, when he reread and commented on the famous page of Pascal's *Pensées* about a man alone in a room, Maine de Biran apparently found himself in exactly the same situation as that described by Pascal. After retreating to his country home with the firm decision to devote himself to study and a life of solitude, sheltered from the distractions of Parisian life and the political turmoil that was sweeping across France, he discovered to his deep disappointment that he was simply incapable of focusing on his task. Not unlike what happened to him in Paris, Maine de Biran found himself prone to distraction, constantly led astray and in need of physical movement. For him it became clear that his inability to concentrate and collect his thoughts was not caused by the whirlwind of the city's commitments and occupations. At the same time, for Maine de Biran it became equally apparent that this inability was not due, as Pascal claimed, to a supposed feeling of existential misery, which one allegedly prefers not to think about by indulging in distraction:

> Pascal goes too far in his consideration of human nature and gives entirely imaginary reasons for the misery felt by a man deprived of movement and activity. He claims that this feeling of misery arises from the reflection that a *degenerate* being would make about himself, when in reality this feeling simply comes from the fact that this mixed being is not purely intellectual and has physical needs that imperatively demand to be satisfied.
>
> (*Journal*, I, 62)

While initially siding with Pascal, Maine de Biran would in fact end up refining Voltaire's criticism. Not only does the isolation of a quiet and secluded life, solely devoted to intellectual or spiritual activity, not suffice to bring about human happiness, but it is simply impossible for human beings to live without engaging in a relationship with what lies outside themselves. This does not prove that humans are *degenerate* beings, as Pascal supposed, but simply shows that they are *mixed* beings, whose animal and sensory parts make them eager for sensation and movement. The need for distraction does not arise from the thought of our mortality, which would assail us in moments of solitude, but is a tendency that is part and parcel of human nature. In other words, this tendency has nothing to do with guilt or sin but derives from the physical and material dimension of our existence—something that Pascal dismisses all too easily.

Maine de Biran's commentary does not even spare Pascal's conception of boredom. The malaise that assails us in times of loneliness has little to do with the metaphysical anguish arising from the consideration of human misery in the universe. For Maine de Biran, boredom has a much more physical than metaphysical nature and is nothing more than "a disease of our physical and moral faculties" in need of sensation, movement, and activities (*Journal*, I, 63). As such, it is close to the pathological state that the medical textbooks of his day referred to as "melancholy."

As Montaigne himself had been quick to realize when he decided to live secluded in the most complete idleness, for Maine de Biran too the torment that a man feels in solitude, without anything to distract him, is not of an intellectual nature (it does not arise from the fact that introspection would lead him to meditate on himself), but simply depends on the insuppressible need for life and movement, for the absence of which the mind often compensates by generating an uncontrolled proliferation of images and unregulated thoughts.[3] This is how Maine de Biran reformulates Pascal's motif of the man left alone in a room: "All my trouble comes from the simple fact of being unable to remain calm in a room, whether in Paris or in the country, and of being unable to be master of my own movement" (*Journal*, I, 42). As in Montaigne, the movement Biran refers to is not only physical motion, which the body often performs without our consent, but also the spiritual kind, linked to thought and imagination, which often escapes our will.

However, if Montaigne openly surrenders to his own weakness, deciding to write down, as they arise, the scattered thoughts that occupy his mind in his solitude (the alleged aim being to shame his mind by showing it the bizarre things in which it loses itself),[4] Maine de Biran searches in vain for a technique to control his thoughts and imagination. On the one hand, he seeks a strong occupation to cling to: "reading or leafing through a great quantity of books to satisfy vain curiosity is not an occupation; in so doing, one ends up increasing the mobility of one's imagination, tormenting and agitating oneself in indeterminacy" (*Journal*, I, 123–4). It is possible that he was thinking here precisely of Montaigne, lost among the books in his library. On the other hand, he resorts to the idea of God and religion, though not so much with a view to salvation in the afterlife, as Pascal did, but rather as a form of inner discipline to overcome as far as possible sensory nature, to contain "bad imaginations", and to curb his mind's tendency toward distraction.[5]

5. Assault on the "Inner Citadel"

The unstable and changeable nature of our self, already stressed by Montaigne, was no longer a novelty for those who, like Maine de Biran, had gone through the revolution brought about by Locke and sensationism with regard to the conception of human nature. This paradigm shift had highlighted how, from both a gnoseological and a moral point of view, our being is nothing more than the ever-changing result of sensory experience and the set of relations that bind us to the outside world. Even Voltaire and Rousseau could only agree on this point. As Rousseau observes in *Les Confessions*—repeating an idea that we have already found in the *Lettres philosophiques*, but giving greater prominence to the unconscious character of this process:

> By probing myself and by seeking in others what [our] different manners of being depended on, I found that in large part they depended on the prior impression of external objects, and that—since we are continuously modified by our senses and our organs—in our ideas, in our feelings, in our very actions we carried the effect of these modifications without being aware of it.[1]

It was on the basis of this observation that Rousseau conceived the project of writing a book, which he never completed, entitled *La morale sensitive, ou le matérialisme du sage* (Sensitive Morality or the Wise Man's Materialism), in which he proposed to search systematically for the causes of our changes in order to acquire greater control over ourselves, our actions, and our judgments.[2] In other words, the idea was to identify in advance the things that normally drive us, in an attempt to manage them and to minimize the influence of the external environment, anticipating what would otherwise distract us.

Maine de Biran fully embraced this project sketched out by Rousseau, whom he reproached only for failing to consider, in addition to the external causes (colors, sounds, climates, seasons, food, etc.), the internal material causes of our variations and distractions, linked to our temperament and organic sensibility[3]: indeed, unbeknownst to us, these are the things that continuously determine the emotional nuance through which we perceive some objects, places, or situations. Maine de Biran used the term "organic refraction" to describe this phenomenon, in many ways comparable to what Leibniz had tried to identify by speaking of "small" or "obscure perceptions," which represent the unperceived background of all conscious experience. And it is based on this phenomenon that Maine de Biran explains the mutability through which we perceive nature, which sometimes appears to us cheerful and serene, at other times covered by a mournful veil, for no other reason than the variability of our internal affective dispositions. Unconsciously associated with the exercise of the senses and thought, these organic dispositions, which can often vary according to external circumstances, "impregnat[e] things or the colored images that seem to belong to them." It is for this reason that, at different times, the same things can be reasons for hope and love or objects of hatred and fear: "Each age of life, each season of the year, sometimes each of the hours of the day sees the contrast of these intimate modes of our sensory being."[4]

A similar phenomenon would later be noted by Giacomo Leopardi with regard to the experience of reading. The "I" or subjectivity of the reader changes not only from year to year, month to month, or day to day but can also vary greatly in the course of a single day for very different reasons—"internal and external, physical and mental, [...] temporary or lasting"—which dispose the reader's mind or imagination differently. The influence of such minute factors, which escape our conscious attention, is such that often "a man varies considerably in his estimation of works of equal value, and even the same work, at different times of life, under different circumstances, and even at different hours of the day,"[5] so that a page that had thrilled us in the morning may leave us completely indifferent if we reread it in the evening.

So we should not be surprised that it is often chance that determines our most important choices. As much as we like to pretend otherwise, especially in the narratives through which we rationally reconstruct a posteriori particular junctures of our past, in reality, if we think about it, there is never a moment in which we can say with unshakable certainty "this is what I think, this is what I want." We can never be sure that some extrinsic factor (the temperature of the air, a gloomy day, poor digestion, a change in the light, somebody's tone of voice, the fleeting impression of a glance, or even just the interference of an involuntary memory) has not indirectly influenced the course of our thoughts or the inclination of our will. If Cleopatra's nose had been shorter, Pascal himself acknowledges, the face of the earth would probably not be the same today (*Pensées*, 32).[6]

Whether these causes of distraction lie within or outside us is actually quite secondary. What's more important is the fact that they escape our consciousness as well as our will. Viewed from this perspective, the problem of distraction no longer concerns the dialectic between inside and outside, between interiority and exteriority, but rather the relationship between the sphere of the voluntary and the much broader sphere of the involuntary. The latter includes all those movements—be they physical or spiritual, produced by external or internal causes—that we cannot control and which consequently render us incapable of exercising free thought.

Marcus Aurelius, the Stoic philosopher upon whose teaching Maine de Biran had initially based his own self-discipline, believed that it is not external things that come toward us but we who go toward them, according to a movement that could be defined as distraction and over which we have full control. Although, as we have seen, Pascal was less confident than the Stoics about the possibility of finding salvation by relying on our own strength, he still believed that a return to interiority, safe from external distractions, was possible. What began to waver, especially with Rousseau, was the idea that we have control over this movement toward external things. Indeed, the question began to arise as to whether it is not things themselves that come toward us, penetrating our interiority *without us being aware of it*. What faded away, then, was the belief in the primacy of the moral and intellectual order over the physical, which is why the only thing we can do, for Rousseau, is to try to establish it indirectly, by forcing external objects and the physical disposition of our body to favor a moral order that they would otherwise constantly upset.

Maine de Biran's conclusions, as we have seen, are even more radical. What distracts us, making us lose control over ourselves, our actions, thoughts, and judgements, is not only found outside of us but also *inside* us. This undermines another important teaching of Marcus Aurelius, namely the idea that, when we are afflicted by something external, it is not the thing itself that upsets us, but the judgement we place on it. The problem, for Maine de Biran, is precisely this: because of "organic refraction," over which neither philosophy nor virtue has any power, it is no longer so obvious that we can make this distinction, that is, that we can separate things from the judgement we make of them and the qualities we attribute to them according to the variability of our affective dispositions.

Interiority—which for Marcus Aurelius was an inviolable remnant of freedom, the "citadel" guarded by the will, whose boundaries could not be crossed by external things without our consent[7]—is now under siege from all sides, assaulted not only from the outside but also from within the body and the organism itself. What remains to be considered is whether we can see what appears to be a defeat as the starting point for a different approach to the problem of distraction.

6. Chasing a Hare: Pascal on the Unpleasant Use of Pleasure

As we have seen, Pascal uses the term "divertissement" in two different but related senses. "Divertissement" means, first of all, all that distracts us—that is, any activity, engagement, occupation, or use of time by which we avoid thinking about more important things. But "divertissement" also refers to the mechanism, of which we are mostly unaware, that leads us to distraction.

While criticizing the conduct of those who, like the libertines, adopt *divertissement* as a philosophy of life, Pascal's analysis of this phenomenon is all but a blank condemnation. In his view, the behavior of ordinary people, who instinctively indulge in *divertissement*, deserves to be taken much more seriously than philosophers normally do. If our condition were truly happy, we would not need to forget about it through *divertissement* in order to be happy (*Pensées*, 104 and 165).

According to Pascal, the error of those who seek happiness through *divertissement* is not so much a matter of substance but rather of judgement. This mistake consists in behaving as if achieving whatever one tirelessly pursues in one's daily activities—be it a ball or money, a boar or a hare, an important position or the favors of a loved one—should make one happy. Instead, such activities are merely a diversion from thinking about unhappiness, masking the actual emptiness of the pleasure these things can offer. Although they correspond to a legitimate wish for happiness, such pleasures will never be able to satisfy us because they come from outside and are subject to a thousand contingencies which do not depend on us and which we cannot control. To be truly happy—happy according to the measure of one's desire—one would need something that is both stable and permanent.

That is why, as Pascal points out, in *divertissement* "we never seek things for themselves, only the pursuit of them"; we enjoy "the chase, and not the quarry," games more than victory, and disputes more than truth itself (*Pensées*, 637 and 168). In fact, none of us seriously believes that the happiness to which we aspire consists in catching the hare we are hunting or in getting the money we might win at gambling. For if these things which we seek so ardently were offered to us directly, without the business of the chase or the hazard of the challenge, we would not want them, as they would then reveal their emptiness and would no longer save us from boredom. But we are not aware of this mechanism: if we were to play cards without staking money, we would be bored. A purposeless agitation is not enough to divert us from unhappiness.

In order for these occupations to be effective sources of distraction, human beings have to get excited, they have to deceive themselves and imagine that they would be happy if they achieved what they are after. The disappointment that invariably pervades us once we have achieved our goal is not enough to convince us of the illusory nature of our projects and dreams. This is because, as Pascal explains, illuminating a decisive psychological mechanism at play in the human mind's own process of illusion, the cases and examples we have before our eyes are never perfectly identical: the slight differences that occur between different instances over time give us hope that the next opportunity will finally be the right one and that our expectations will not be disappointed—not this time. It is in this way that, deceived by experience, "from one failure to another," we finally come to death (*Pensées*, 181).

This confused and contradictory dynamic that takes shape in the pursuit of *divertissement* is interpreted by Pascal as the result of two "secret instincts." The first instinct leads us to search for happiness by pouring ourselves outward, exhausting ourselves in the noise and tumult of occupations that prevent us from thinking about ourselves and our own nothingness. The second instinct, on the contrary, makes us realize that the happiness we seek can only consist in the quiet and rest offered by something stable and lasting. While the first instinct confusingly grasps something true, though without fully appreciating the meaning of this truth, the second instinct is instead "a remnant of the greatness of our original nature," the hidden trace of an emptiness left in us by a happiness we have lost. This emptiness, being infinite, can only be filled by "an infinite, immutable object," namely God himself (*Pensées*, 168 and 181).

But how do we know that this aspiration toward infinity, which nourishes our longing for happiness, is actually the sign of a condition from which we have fallen? How do we know it is not simply—as other thinkers less troubled by religious concerns would argue—a figment of our imagination? Pascal himself was well aware of the power that the imagination wields over the human mind and the traps it can set even for the wisest of us. As experience teaches us every day, he observes, not only does the imagination prevail over reason far more often than we would like, but it can overcome sensation itself, which it is able to suspend or alter according to the temptations of desire. Imagination's greatest deception comes from the fact that "while it is most often false, it gives no indication of its quality, indicating in the same way both truth and falsehood" (*Pensées*, 78).

Pascal nevertheless places a limit on the deceptive power of the imagination. It is this limit that allows him to avoid the skeptical doubts of the Pyrrhonians without falling into the dogmatism of their opponents. Returning to a classic argument, inaugurated by Plato to prove the immortality of the soul and which Augustine had later adapted to the Christian context,[1] Pascal observes that ideas that we cannot have derived from experience must necessarily come from elsewhere: this makes them the proof of a previous condition that has fallen into oblivion. In Pascal's own words, "if man had never been other than corrupted, he would have no notion of either truth or beatitude" (*Pensées*, 164). Although incapable of either, humans cannot help but desire happiness and truth. This desire must therefore be a sign of where we come from, a way to "make us realize where we have fallen from" (*Pensées*, 20). That is why the lack that we experience through the desire for stable and inexhaustible happiness is not an illusion but the mark of a fullness and perfection that we have lost.

One often gets the impression, reading Pascal's *Pensées*, that some aspects of human nature condemned or pitied as examples of human corruption actually correspond to genuine psychological and anthropological discoveries whose scope goes far beyond Pascal's pessimism. This is particularly true with regard to the analysis of *divertissement*. One of Pascal's great discoveries in this respect consists in having grasped how this strategy that "men have managed to invent to make themselves happy" (*Pensées*, 168) is based on an unpleasant use of pleasure itself, employed not as an end but as a means of masking the emptiness of all possible pleasures and the actual dissatisfaction they bring us.[2] What we really look for (albeit unconsciously, by means of a "secret instinct") in all the amusement, occupations, or activities by which we distract ourselves every day is not so much the pleasure or satisfaction they provide us with per se but rather their capacity for diversion and continuous opening toward the future. Pascal gave this discovery a negative connotation and viewed it as the root of human misery: "the present is never our end. Past and present are our means, only the future is our end. And so we never actually live, though we hope to, and in constantly striving for happiness it is inevitable we will never achieve it" (*Pensées*, 80). But this retreat into an anthropological pessimism with a theological origin in no way detracts from the significance of this discovery which, once separated from the moral and apologetic framework in which Pascal places it, can perhaps be turned into something positive.

7. The "Theory of Pleasure": Leopardi between Pascal and Montaigne

We could define the "theory of pleasure" that Giacomo Leopardi expounds in his intellectual journal, the *Zibaldone*, as a secularized reinterpretation of Pascal's *divertissement*. Leopardi's premises are indeed not different from Pascal's. Since human desire aims at the infinite, boredom and dissatisfaction are always lurking in every pleasure. If Pascal compared boredom to a poison that fills the spirit as soon as we are left alone with ourselves (*Pensées*, 168), Leopardi saw boredom as the air that filters through a spider's web. Just as air is quick to fill the empty spaces between material things, so boredom fills the emptiness of all pleasures.

For Leopardi boredom is less about thought and more about desire, of which it is an extreme manifestation. Boredom is nothing more than the negative reverse of our yearning for infinity, the feeling that arises in us from experiencing the disproportion between imagined and real pleasure, the unbridgeable gap between desire and any possible satisfaction. In this sense, boredom is the "pure desire for happiness" that we experience as such in the very moment of pleasure, when it reveals its inconsistency with respect to the expectation of desire.[1]

That is why against boredom there is no other remedy than distraction—a distraction that, as Pascal already explained, prevents one from perceiving the inconsistency of real pleasures by making an unpleasant use of pleasure itself, employed not so much as an end but as a means to distract our desire: "And this is the best and most truly pleasurable effect of human and animal pleasure: to occupy the mind and—not to satisfy desire, which is impossible—but in part, and in a certain way, to distract it almost, stuffing its throat like insatiable Cerberus and his sop." Or else: "I consider the things called pleasures to be useful and leading to happiness, only insofar as they are strong distractions, and lively diversions of self-love—because they are of no use in any other way."[2]

As Leopardi points out, taking his cue from one of Pascal's thoughts, pleasure or happiness always lies in the future, never in the present; they do not consist in achieving a specific goal (for instance, owning a horse) but are given only in the hope or expectation of pleasure—that is in desire itself.[3] It is for this reason that an occupation as pleasurable as reading invariably leads to boredom when we seek in it no other end than present enjoyment or pursue it as a mere pastime, without any future purpose. Pascal had observed something similar about travel, which fatally ceases to be pleasurable as soon as we subordinate the very pleasure of traveling to the pleasure of recounting our journey and begin to concentrate on the present satisfaction we expect to derive from it.[4] For reading and traveling to be distracting and enjoyable occupations, they must be accompanied by the hope of some future pleasure that depends on them and distracts us from the present:

> [M]an is not intrinsically capable of any noteworthy pleasure that does not consist first of all in hope, the power of which is such that many occupations unpleasant in themselves, and even boring and wearisome and however time consuming, become most pleasant and joyful, provided the expectations of some good result is added to them. Conversely, whatever is thought to be pleasurable in itself

becomes boring if it is deprived of hope almost as soon as, so to speak, it is tasted.[5]

Thus, any activity driven by a future purpose is in itself much more pleasurable than amusements as such, whose goal is no more than present pleasure (*Zibaldone*, 248). Invented to produce distraction, pastimes or amusements miss precisely the essential point of distraction, which consists in occupying the mind and distracting desire, without leaving us time to reflect on the impossibility of obtaining the pleasure we strive for (*Zibaldone*, 173).[6]

However, while starting from the same premises as Pascal, Leopardi reaches opposite conclusions. The need for infinity inscribed in desire, which for Pascal was the trace of our true origin and destination, becomes instead in Leopardi a simple product of the human mind. It is this change of perspective that, by freeing the device of *divertissement* from Pascal's moral and transcendent assumptions, allows Leopardi to consider it solely from an ethical point of view and to explore its vital scope. Since there is no happiness other than that which human beings have been able to come up with through distraction (a happiness that lies more in desire than in possession, more in the imagination of pleasure than in pleasure itself), we are allowed to pursue it in every possible way.[7]

Moreover, as Leopardi points out in a move reminiscent of Montaigne, distraction is a stratagem employed by nature itself. This same stratagem is at work every time that nature pleasantly confuses our imagination by giving us the illusion of the infinite through the indefinite, by way of the multiplicity, variety, or boundless extension of objects. Thus, without leaving us time to reflect on the finitude of every possible pleasure, it makes us "switch rapidly from one thing to another," from sensation to sensation, from desire to desire. In Leopardi's "History of the Human Race," distraction is indeed one of the means by which Jupiter, just like nature, sought to make up for the impossibility of attaining endless pleasure—a pleasure that is nowhere to be found but which humankind nevertheless desires (*Zibaldone*, 167–9).

It is as if in the "theory of pleasure," which is in fact nothing but a theory of distraction, Leopardi had found a way to reconcile Montaigne and Pascal—to revisit, in the spirit of Montaigne, the scope of Pascal's discovery.

Part Two

The Power of Flies

Avant-propos

Contrary to what our confident reason may lead us to believe, we are not quite so in control of our attention as we wish. This simple fact is easy to observe. We don't need the deafening roar of a motorbike speeding down the road or the dazzling light of a lamp suddenly turning on to divert the course of our thoughts, capturing our whole attention in an instant. As we well know, the most trivial things are often enough to distract us from what we are doing. When we are absorbed in reading or in thought, the steady dripping of a tap or the obstinate ticking of a clock often have the singular ability to immobilize our minds, stripping us of any ability to focus them elsewhere. Indeed, it even appears that the more feeble and almost imperceptible these stimuli are, the more despotic their power over our attention. Someone's quiet whispering in the library, the intermittent hissing of a household appliance, or the slight creaking of a chair often disturb us more than the continuous crackling of a radio, the alternating noise of traffic, or the scattered chatter at a street market. If a constant racket can paradoxically favor concentration by pushing our thoughts inward,[1] discontinuous sounds—even if quiet—seem to attract our attention more powerfully, poking and prodding it in spite of ourselves. Just like an insect caught in a spider's web, which gets more entangled the more it struggles, trying not to think about what's distracting us already means thinking about it. In cases like these, there appears to be no other solution than to surrender to distraction, possibly leaving to habit the task of gradually anaesthetizing our senses and soundproofing the rooms we live in.

For centuries, meditation exercises—initially reserved for the solitude of monasteries but now so widespread as to be practiced on dedicated apps—have taught us how to train our minds to acquire progressive control over our attention. The technological invasion, which is gaining more and more space in everyday life, seems to make us more exposed to distraction, yet it would be naive to think of it as the primary cause of this problem. Despite being often accused of producing an irreversible anthropological mutation, technology actually adds nothing to the mechanism of distraction. Rather, it acts as a magnifier that makes certain aspects or tendencies of human nature more evident and manifest.[2] Manuals such as *The Imitation of Christ*, a veritable handbook of rules and exercises aimed at keeping monks' attention constantly turned to God, remind us that distraction comes first and foremost from the body and the imagination. This is why the anonymous author invited the religious person to close "the door of [their] sense"[3] because it is from there that the devil has access to our soul, instilling sensations and images that distract us from spiritual things.[4] In a way, in the contemporary imagination, technology plays the same role as the tempting devil did for monks in the Middle Ages: it is only the generic name under which we understand a broader cause.

On closer inspection, the phenomenology of distraction does not appear to have substantially changed since the fifteenth century (but one could go back even further):

> Oh, what inward suffering I undergo when I consider heavenly things; when I pray, a multitude of carnal thoughts rush upon me! [...] For I confess truly that I am accustomed to be very much distracted. Very often I am not where bodily I stand or sit; rather, I am where my thoughts carry me.
>
> (*The Imitation of Christ*, III, ch. 48, 214–15)

At first sight, one might think that distraction points to a radical dualism between mind and body, with the latter remaining still while thought wanders elsewhere. However, it actually attests to their indissoluble and inextricable unity. Perhaps if we did not have a body, if our existence were completely separate from matter, we would be able to govern our thoughts promptly and at all times. Angels, whom the Christian tradition imagines as incorporeal beings, have no knowledge of distraction[5] (and yet in Wim Wenders's film *Wings of Desire*, it is by secretly listening to the scattered thoughts of human beings that an angel begins to wish to be one of them).

In contrast, animals, like children, are very easily distracted: their whole body shows this. Just observe a cat for a few minutes and you'll see how promptly it obeys the slightest deviations of attention. Its ears stand up at every noise, its head quickly turns around, and its paw immediately leaps forward. If a cat is caught up in some sensation that suddenly captures the attention, its muscles are stretched, ready to jump in a given direction or run away in the opposite one. Conversely, humans, unable to be in control of their attention, have trained the body (at least!) to remain still. This is the first skill children are expected to acquire at school, where they learn to sit meekly at their desk for hours, despite the tempting call of voices coming from outside, the sun shining through the window, or the passing of a cloud. And yet, as Pascal observes, not even someone firm and severe like a judge is exempt from distraction: if they go to church and see that the preacher is badly shaven or has a hoarse voice, they will be unable to stop their imagination from wandering, despite remaining physically motionless in their seat (Pascal, *Pensées*, 78).

1. Augustine and Pascal

Augustine was one of the first to portray the fragility of our attention, providing examples later taken up by Pascal among others.[1] Paradoxically, as Augustine observes, the spirit governs the body much more easily than it governs itself (*Confessions*, VIII, 9.21).[2] It is easier to move an arm, unless some physical obstacle prevents us from doing so, than to direct the course of our thoughts. Just where will and power should be as one, we experience an embarrassing disconnection: it is as if the spirit wanted and did not want at the same time. The cause of this paradox, of this impairment and "sickness of the mind" (*Confessions*, VIII, 9.21) that lets itself be dragged here and there randomly and inconsistently, is to be found in original sin.

It is for disobeying the divine commandment, eating the only forbidden fruit, that Adam and Eve, and the entire humankind with them, have been punished by becoming slaves to the body and the flesh, incapable of exercising their will in an absolute and undivided manner: "This condemnation was such that man [*homo*], who would have been spiritual even in flesh if he had observed the order, became carnal in mind as well" (*The City of God*, XIV, 15.1). Even the highest and most immaterial part of human nature became subjugated to the body and to the sensory world; against its own will the mind started to be agitated by stimuli, passions, and impulses coming from the body and often causing a "total eclipse of acumen" (*The City of Good*, XIV, 16). Having become mortal, humankind fell prey to involuntary bodily movements that affect the spirit and was reduced to a condition in which "man disagrees with himself and leads a life of cruel and wretched slavery, under the rule of the one with whom he agreed when he sinned" (*The City of God*, XIV, 15.1). That is why, as Augustine explains in *De libero arbitrio*, "all sins are contained under this one heading, when someone turns aside from divine and genuinely abiding things and towards changeable and uncertain things."[3] Distraction from God, initially caused by pride and then irreparable, is the origin of all sins and contains their essence. This is how, through distraction, the devil has become able to control our spirit through the body, as illustrated in the allegorical reading of original sin offered in *De trinitate*: the bodily senses, symbolized by the serpent, seduce Eve (lust), who in turn corrupts Adam (reason, the will) by dragging him into corruption.[4]

With a bit of awkwardness, in Book X of *The Confessions* Augustine admits that his life, even after the great turning point of his conversion, is still miserably filled with episodes of distraction. Futile thoughts, often insinuated by external stimuli that suddenly captured his attention, constantly interrupt his prayers or distract him from important reflections. Human existence is so contaminated by the body and the flesh, so captivated by the sensory world, that the most irrelevant things—a dog chasing after a hare or a spider catching a fly in its web—are enough to capture our attention:

> I do not watch a hound chasing past a hare when it takes place at the circus; but if it happens in an open field, and I happen to be passing, that pursuit grips my attention and diverts my thoughts from some weighty reflection onto itself. It is not the physical movement of my horse, but my heart's propensity, that forces a change of course. Once my own weakness has been made clear to me, you quickly warn me that unless I use the sight of that spectacle to produce some kind of reflection that helps me to ascend to you (or to dismiss the sight and move on) I become less receptive, a vain creature. What about when I am sitting at home and the sight of a lizard catching flies, or a spider entangling anything that blunders into its webs, often has me riveted?
>
> (*Confessions*, X, 35.57)

Even more so than the initial example of a dog chasing a hare, this last series of examples (a lizard catching flies or a spider trapping insects in its web) is particularly apt to show the fragility and fickleness of human attention, which is also—or rather, above all—distracted by the smallest and most insignificant things. We are so incapable of directing the course of our thoughts that anything is enough to distract us.

Pascal describes the same phenomenon when, in the *Pensées*, he ironically alludes to the subtle "power of flies" (*Pensées*, 56). Apparently harmless, these little insects actually have the extraordinary ability to paralyze our mind, making us incapable of thinking or making a good decision. The fact is, as Pascal explains:

> The mind of this sovereign judge of the world is not so independent that it cannot be disturbed by the first nearby clatter. It does not need a cannon's roar to immobilize its thoughts, the noise of a weathervane or a pulley will do. Do not be surprised if he cannot gather his thoughts at the moment—a fly is buzzing in his ear. That is enough to make him incapable of giving sound advice. If you want him to reach the truth, then chase away the insect holding his reason in check, disturbing that mighty intellect which rules over cities and kingdoms.
>
> (*Pensées*, 81)

For Pascal, as we have seen in Part One, the fact that even a ball thrown around or a wild boar running during a hunt are enough to distract us from the deepest pains is a remarkable sign of human frivolity (*Pensées*, 453). But the fact that things as trivial as the creaking of a pulley or the buzzing of a fly can take away all our concentration is for him even more upsetting. Furthermore, if we can get used to the continuous noise of a pulley until we almost do not hear it anymore, no habit seems able to protect our concentration against the stubborn and discontinuous buzzing of an insect, which will never cease to exert an irresistible power of distraction over us. Even Montaigne, who, perched in his tower, had grown accustomed to the noise produced by a large bell that regularly tolled the *Ave Maria* twice a day, shaking the entire building (*Essais*, I, ch. 23), confessed that he could not resist the power of the flies: "I have a mind which is delicate and easy to distract: when it withdraws aside to concentrate, the least buzzing of a fly is enough to murder it!" (*Essais*, III, ch. 13, Fr. 1082, Eng. 1228).

Perhaps it is no coincidence that precisely the buzzing of flies, a distractive element par excellence from Montaigne to Pascal and in devotional literature,[5] would be defined by the narrator of Marcel Proust's *À la recherche du temps perdu* (In Search of Lost Time)—more inclined, as we shall see, toward the power of distraction—as the symphony of his summers, accompanying his reading afternoons as a child. As much as a distraction, the buzzing of flies becomes part of the narrator's experience, encapsulating the essence of the summer and his "feeling of the day's brightness and splendor":

> the flies who performed for my benefit, in their tiny chorus, as it were the chamber music of summer; evoking heat and light quite differently from an air of human music which, if you happen to have heard it during a fine summer, will always bring that summer back to your mind, the music of the flies is bound to the season by a closer, a more compelling tie—born of the sunny days, and not to be reborn but with them, containing something of their essential nature, it not merely calls up their image in our memory, but gives us a guarantee that they do really exist, that they are close around us, immediately accessible.[6]

2. Serendipity

We might perhaps believe, as the philosopher Étienne Bonnot de Condillac jokingly observed, that an insect is not worthy of taking up more space in a scholar's mind than it does in nature and that only large objects, such as mountains, heavenly bodies, and the expanses of the sea, have a right to occupy the spacious foreheads of scientists.[1]

Yet, according to a well-known anecdote, the invention of the Cartesian coordinate system is due to a fly which, fluttering on the ceiling of Descartes's bedroom, gave the father of modern rationalism the idea of describing its trajectory by taking the corners of the walls as reference points. According to Colerus's account, one of Spinoza's favorite pastimes was watching spiders and flies fighting, and he enjoyed examining gnats and mosquitoes under a microscope.[2] It would be a mistake to think that these apparently puerile amusements have little to do with the philosopher's geometrical rigor: in its dense interweaving of references and internal connections, Spinoza's *Ethics* is very much constructed like a spiderweb.[3] And precisely the example of spiders is used by Spinoza to exemplify some key ideas in his philosophy, such as the relativity of the idea of perfection[4] or the incommensurability of the powers relative to each being: just as a spider, Spinoza observes, weaves with a dexterity that not even the most expert tailor would ever be able to replicate, so it is possible that humans may be able to do things that angels cannot.[5]

Distraction, such as that caused by the buzzing of a fly, has traditionally been seen as a defect to be corrected, as a threatening power that besieges us on all sides. But is it really true that distraction is something we must protect ourselves against or escape from? Sometimes, on the contrary, precisely what distracts us gives rise to some encounter or discovery that we had not foreseen. This phenomenon is so well known that it has been given a name. The term "serendipity," according to the definition provided by the writer and antiquarian Horace Walpole, who introduced this neologism in 1754, indicates precisely the unforeseen discoveries made "by accident and sagacity" and which would never have been accomplished if we had always remained attentive and focused on what we were doing—that is, if we had not listened to what was distracting us.

It is often forgotten that Augustine's conversion, narrated in Book VIII of *The Confessions*, started precisely from a moment of distraction. If Augustine had not let himself be distracted by a child singing in a nearby house, he would never have opened the book in front of him and would not have been struck by the first passage by St. Paul that his eyes fell on.[6] Of course, given the apologetic intentions of *The Confessions*, Augustine cannot but frame the whole story in the perspective of Providence: it is God himself who, in his grace, has arranged it all, aware that human weakness needs external stimuli and exhortations from the sensory world.[7] The possibility of random discoveries, made by using lateral or oblique thinking while being distracted by something secondary, is foreign to late antique and medieval thought. Even purely coincidental perceptions were considered, in the words of Thomas Aquinas, examples of "infused virtue" as God-given gifts.[8] In this sense, as the author of *The Confessions* observes, addressing God, "your ideal servants are those who no longer look to hear from you the answer that they want, but instead want what they hear from you" (*Confessions*, X, 26). And yet there is no doubt that through the story of his conversion, Augustine created the palimpsest of all the events that, from what are called serendipities to the illuminations of Poincaré or Proust, would highlight the importance of distraction, which sometimes proves to be indispensable to make decisive discoveries or to find what we are looking for. God, Augustine already seems to tell us, is in the details.[9]

3. A Distracted Mathematician: Poincaré and the Role of Distraction in Invention

Those who set out on a journey after choosing their destination do not need to keep their minds fixed on the point of arrival to reach it: in the same way—observes Pierre Nicole by criticizing the rigor with which Pascal considers the phenomenon of distraction— once a certain intention has been formed (for example to love and serve God), it is not necessary to think about it continuously for it to remain the ultimate guiding light of our thoughts and actions.[1] After all, experience teaches us that thinking assiduously about something we want to achieve is not only impossible—because of the material implication of our existence, which exposes us inevitably and imperiously to distraction—but also counterproductive. What we are stubbornly and unsuccessfully looking for (a name on the tip of our tongue, the solution to a problem that is bothering us) cannot always—in fact it almost never can—be found through a prolonged effort of our attention. More often than not, the solution we are looking for or the name that is eluding us suddenly comes to mind at the exact moment when we stop thinking about it and let ourselves be distracted by something else.

It is said that Archimedes discovered how to measure the volume of an irregular solid—a problem he had been racking his brains over for days and to whose solution we owe the famous cry "Eureka!"—by immersing himself in his bathtub: it was then that he realized that the amount of water overflowing was equal to the volume of his own body.[2] True or not, this anecdote (on a par with Newton's apple) captures an essential aspect of the way our mind works. More particularly, it showcases the decisive role played by the interaction between chance and intelligence, as well as between the conscious and the unconscious, made possible by distraction. On the one hand, by diverting conscious attention from a certain problem, we allow the solution to take shape spontaneously at the margins of consciousness, as in a sort of decanting or spontaneous maturation of ideas. On the other hand, it can also happen that precisely what is distracting us provides the opportunity to come unexpectedly across the solution, through paths that we would have been unable to conceive of rationally.

During a lecture at the Société de Psychologie in Paris, later published in 1908 in the volume *Science et méthode* (Science and Method), the mathematician Henri Poincaré recounted how some of his most brilliant intuitions occurred in the most unlikely and unpredictable circumstances. During a geological outing, a totally unpredictable intuition suddenly struck him at the exact moment when he put his foot on a step while entering an omnibus. On a short holiday at the seaside, the solution he had been looking for unsuccessfully dawned on him while he was taking a walk along the cliff, intent on thinking about something else.[3] In both cases, Poincaré tells us, not only was his conscious attention elsewhere, but his mind was expressly inclined toward the opposite solution. By suspending for a moment the goals that the mind consciously sets itself, the distraction allowed him to test possibilities contrary to those toward which his mind was intentionally directed and which his conscious self would never have admitted or contemplated. Illuminations such as these punctuate the careers of many mathematicians and scientists, and Poincaré derives from them a whole theory concerning the role of distraction in the "psychological mechanism of invention." For a discovery to be made, intense initial preparatory work, carried out without apparent results and then abruptly interrupted, must be followed by a relatively long period of rest. The crucial idea may then suddenly emerge while we are intent on doing something else or may spontaneously pop up when we go back to work.

We are all familiar with this phenomenon and often experience it even in the most trivial of circumstances. Washing dishes or walking to the bus stop, we suddenly find the idea we were looking for or the right turn of phrase to complete the translation of a passage. Or else, we go to bed troubled by a problem that seems to have no solution, but in the morning, reconsidering things in another light, we realize that the way out has been there all along. We generally tend to explain such phenomena by praising the virtues of rest: a temporary suspension of activity seems essential to give the mind the vigor and freshness needed to complete a job or make a decision. Immanuel Kant recommended that people who are very busy should practice the "art of distraction" on a regular basis: thinking about a certain subject all the time is tiring and can lead to madness because it leaves an echo or resonance that is difficult to get rid of, much like a catchy song. Practiced in a moderate and controlled way, distraction then becomes an indispensable measure to guarantee mental health. By shifting the mind's attention elsewhere, it restores the balance of psychic forces and gives us new energy for work and for our usual activities.[4]

For Poincaré, however, things are more complicated than that. During rest, when the conscious attention is shifted elsewhere, the work of the mind is not interrupted at all but continues unconsciously, by inertia, as it were, thanks to the movement caused by an intense initial effort, then abruptly interrupted. Ideas continue to stir in the mind, but with more freedom, testing new solutions or different possible combinations. Distraction, in other words, does not bring rest but *incubation*, during which the mind unconsciously and effortlessly continues the process of rumination that will lead to the solution of the problem. For Poincaré, not only is the unconscious mind not at all inferior to the conscious one, but it can be much more ready and effective than the latter; indeed, it often succeeds where the other fails. We are therefore far from the cautious praise of distraction that we find in Kant, who recommended a temporary and periodic relaxation of the mind as a form of "mental hygiene" suitable for restoring the productive forces of the spirit. In emphasizing the importance of distraction, Kant, unlike Poincaré, neither challenges nor questions the primacy of the conscious self and logical-rational thinking. Kant simply prescribes a moderate and instrumental use of distraction as a form of relaxation that the mind needs from time to time and that, through an industrious alternation of work and rest, makes us more efficient and willing in our normal occupations.

If distraction plays a decisive role in the process of invention described by Poincaré, it is not as a form of recreation, relaxation, or rest but as an indispensable condition for the mind to escape for a moment the vigilant surveillance of the conscious self. At the beginning of the fifth century, the monk John Cassian compared the virtuous soul of a religious man to an officer in charge of supervising soldiers or to a money changer who carefully examines every coin to make sure it is not counterfeit.[5] Borrowing this image, we could say that the conscious self orders the flow of our thoughts like a conscientious guardian, who only lets through familiar ideas. But in so doing, Poincaré seems to suggest, it blocks the way for other insights that could yield unexpected solutions, solutions which are inconceivable according to a logical way of thinking. Were we always to follow logic, Poincaré writes in *La valeur de la science* (The Value of Science), we would find nothing but tautologies: we would never discover anything new.[6] On the contrary, in the absence of a conscious self, the goals that we expressly set ourselves in conducting a certain activity are as if suspended, temporarily forgotten, and it is precisely from this suspension or forgetfulness that the creative scope of distraction arises. It is probably in this sense that we should understand Diderot's observation, according to which a person of ingenuity (*un bon esprit*) must be capable of distraction without being distracted all the time.[7]

To describe the movement, invisible to consciousness, with which ideas stir in the mind in moments of distraction—a movement so chaotic and unpredictable that it can sometimes lead us to discover the opposite of what we were intentionally looking for—Poincaré uses a series of images borrowed from the microscopic world of entomology and the physics of gases.[8] The elements of future combinations are first imagined as "the hooked atoms of Epicurus." When the mind is at complete rest, these atoms lie motionless, as if hanging on the walls of the mind. However, as soon as the process of invention is triggered, some of them, unhooked from the wall, begin to twirl in every direction, in a confused dance that leads them to bump into each other like "a swarm of gnats" locked in a room or to bounce from one side of the mind to the other like "gas molecules" in search of a stable configuration. The role of conscious preliminary work is simply to set some of these elements in motion—be they atoms, gnats, or molecules—urging them to break away from the walls and shoot in every possible direction.

4. Distraction and Trains of Thought: Locke and the Lesson of Sensationism

Ancient German legends speak of tiny industrious dwarves who come out at night to complete, with admirable skill, the work left halfway done by people, leaving them astonished to find it all finished in the morning.[1] In a similar way, it seems that the human mind is able to continue unconsciously a course of reasoning or a work undertaken, without the conscious self participating in any way in this process. It is precisely the temporary absence of the self that allows the solution to emerge undisturbed.

Poincaré's anecdotes are reminiscent of some of the stories circulating at the beginning of the nineteenth century about illustrious figures of the time, such as Benjamin Franklin, the brilliant inventor of the lightning rod, and Condillac, the author of the *Traité des sensations* (Treatise on Sensations). These stories were popularized in particular by the French physician and philosopher Pierre Cabanis, known for his *Rapports du physique et du moral de l'homme* (Relations of the Physical and the Moral in Man). According to Cabanis, Franklin used to unravel in his sleep the political matters that plagued him during the day, while Condillac was able to complete in dream the works he abandoned at bedtime. Cabanis's conclusion resembles Poincaré's: "In fact, the mind can continue its research in dreams; it can be led by a certain sequence of reasonings to ideas that it did not have; it can, without its own knowledge, make rapid calculations that unveil the future for it, as it does at every instant when awake."[2]

If in fact—as already argued by Locke and, before him, by Hobbes[3]—thinking means nothing more than connecting the ideas received from the senses, it seems that, after all, consciousness is not so indispensable to the unfolding of this process. In reality we think even when we are not aware of doing so, and we link ideas together without the active or conscious help of the soul. This happens to us in dreams or in states of distraction, awakening from which we often find ourselves in the company of thoughts of unknown origin. Locke, to be sure, would never have admitted this possibility. In *An Essay Concerning Human Understanding*, he is very careful to exclude the hypothesis that we might think without being aware of it and spends long paragraphs discussing the absurdity of such a theory:

> if it be possible, that the soul can, whilst the body is sleeping, have its thinking [...], which the man is not conscious of, nor partakes in: it is certain, that *Socrates* asleep, and *Socrates* awake, is not the same person [...]. For if we take wholly away all consciousness of our actions and sensations [...], it will be hard to know wherein to place personal identity.[4]

Or else:

> they make the soul and the man two persons, who makes the soul think apart, what the man is not conscious of. For, I suppose, nobody will make identity of persons, to consist in the soul's being united to the very same numerical particles of matter: for if that be necessary to identity, 'twill be impossible, in that constant flux of the particles of our bodies, that any man should be the same person, two days, or two moments together.
>
> (*Essay*, II, ch. 1, § 12)[5]

And yet Locke himself admits that there are different degrees of attention in thought: from what is called study or application, "when the mind with great earnestness, and of choice, fixes its view on any *idea*, considers it on all sides, and will not be called off by the ordinary solicitations of other *ideas*," to what corresponds to the states of dream, ecstasy, and reverie, "when *ideas* float in our mind, without any reflection or regard of the understanding" (*Essay*, Book II, ch. XIX, § 1). In such cases, Locke lets slip, the mind "barely observes the train of *ideas*, that succeed in the understanding," and is sometimes so lazy that it even allows these successions or trains of ideas to "pass almost quite undegraded, as faint shadows, that make no impression" (*Essay*, Book II, ch. XIX, § 3).

Of course Locke warned against the spontaneous associations of the mind, made without the active and deliberate direction of the soul, as in dreams or moments of distraction. Built by chance or custom, these disordered and incoherent associations are closer to the rambling reasoning of a madman than to rational thought. However, if we take Locke's anti-innatism to its extreme consequences (as Condillac and his sensationist followers would do[6]) and explain all the faculties and operations of the mind without involving any preexisting active principle, it clearly becomes impossible to distinguish between the connections that the mind forms under the guidance of reflection and simple passive associations. This is why Cabanis, by showing that he has learned the lesson of sensationism, can affirm without hesitation that the mechanical awakening of ideas in dreams or states of distraction does not necessarily imply illogical and irrational connections. On the contrary, without the supervision of the conscious self and the will, not only can the mind perform the same operations that it normally does, but it also sometimes shows even greater power and discernment.

To return to Locke's example, this means that Socrates asleep may well be philosophically shrewder than Socrates awake. In the *Rêve de d'Alembert* (D'Alembert's Dream), Diderot enjoys exploring this possibility by bringing up another philosopher. In this puzzling multivoiced dialogue between a doctor (the physician Bordeu), a servant (the acute Mademoiselle de Lespinasse), and a sleeping philosopher affected by an unusual somniloquy (d'Alembert), d'Alembert becomes in spite of himself an audacious promulgator of materialistic views that he would have been careful not to admit when awake. How is it possible that, while dreaming, the same individual can brood over things so far removed from what they would acknowledge when awake, so far removed that they cannot even remember them in the morning? Is this the same "person" in both cases, when awake and when asleep? Unlike Locke, Diderot does not seem particularly disturbed by the possibility of answering no to this question. Indeed, as he writes, sleep is that state of "anarchy" in which all the threads of the soul "rise up against their commander, there's no longer a supreme authority," and thought, without consciousness, is as if temporarily displaced throughout the body.[7]

It is precisely in this period, at the turn of the nineteenth century, that the possibility of an unconscious and impersonal dimension of thought began to take shape and started to be considered the main source of creativity. The French psychiatrist Paul Chabaneix will call this dimension "subconscious," observable in particular in states of dreaming, somnambulism, hallucination, and distraction (*relâchement de l'attention*, loosening of attention).[8] In his book *Physiologie cérébrale. Le subconscient chez les artistes, les savants et les écrivains* (Cerebral Physiology. The Subconscious in Artists, Scientists, and Writers) (1879), Chabaneix reports several stories that are very similar to those narrated by Cabanis and whose protagonists include Descartes, Voltaire, Goethe, Mozart, Schopenhauer, Tolstoj, La Fontaine, Walter Scott, Hegel, Schiller, and Madame de Staël—all of whom would have experienced the virtues of unconscious creation. As Emmanuel Régis explains in his preface, where he summarizes Chabaneix's thesis, "automatic cerebral activity can generate not only vague and confused reveries, but also uninterrupted reflections, vivid and ordered scenes, sometimes even completed mental products that often appear to the individual to be born outside their will or even outside themselves." Great artists, "lost in their subconscious distraction," are not mad people but "awakened sleepers."[9]

Poincaré, as we saw, shares the idea that the non-conscious self is in no way inferior to the conscious one and that ideas can spontaneously combine and associate in the mind without consciousness or the will taking any part in this process, as in fact happens in moments of distraction. However, Poincaré points out, discoveries do not simply happen in this way. Stories like those reported by Cabanis and Chabaneix risk making us forget the importance of the conscious work that must both *precede* and *follow* the work that is unconscious. A conscious and voluntary effort remains indispensable not only at the beginning, to set the "unconscious machine" in motion and trigger the movement of ideas, but also at the end, when it comes to verifying, evaluating, and exploiting the results obtained. Poincaré writes:

> It never happens that [unconscious work] gives us the result of a somewhat long calculation all made, where we have only to apply fixed rules. We might think the wholly automatic subliminal self [*le moi subliminal*] particularly apt for this sort of work, which is in a way exclusively mechanical. It seems that thinking in the evening upon the factors of a multiplication we might hope to find the product ready made upon our awakening, or again that an algebraic calculation, for example a verification, would be made unconsciously. Nothing of the sort, as observation proves. All one may hope from these inspirations, fruits of unconscious work, is a point of departure for such calculations. As for the calculations themselves, they must be made in the second period of conscious work, that which follows the inspiration, that in which one verifies the results of this inspiration and deduces their consequences. The rules of these calculations are strict and complicated. They require discipline, attention, will, and therefore consciousness.[10]

But there is another, even more decisive difference. According to Poincaré, the process of invention that is triggered in moments of distraction is not something merely automatic, nor does it simply consist in building new combinations from given elements. This could be done by anyone with excellent memory and an exceptional attention span, able to keep in mind a large number of combinations and avoid calculation errors. It is clear not only that a machine would surpass any human brain in this task but also, as Poincaré points out, that most of the combinations thus obtained would be completely devoid of interest. Memory and attention, which make mathematicians similar to good chess players, able to foresee and remember a large number of possible moves, are not enough to make them brilliant inventors. To make great discoveries, the ability to be distracted is much more useful than great memory and attention.

In fact, according to Poincaré, inventing means knowing how *to choose*: how to bring to light, among all possible combinations, only those that prove to be useful and fertile, which are a very small minority. This is obviously a rather paradoxical choice because it is not made voluntarily or rationally, but it imposes itself on consciousness, which can only take note of it in retrospect. This unconscious "choice" takes place thanks to rules that no machine or automatism could reproduce or apply because they cannot be formulated but only "felt." Such a choice, in fact, pertains to a veritable "aesthetic feeling" that is in no way different from that which makes us appreciate beauty and harmony and which requires mathematicians to exercise a somewhat artistic taste or "sensitivity." It is this faculty that allows them to guess the hidden relationships between seemingly distant and disparate things and induces them to choose, among all possible combinations, only those that are more "harmonious," in a proper Leibnizian sense: that is, only those that allow them to explain a complex problem in the simplest way and to bring order where disorder seemed to reign.

5. What Is Essential Is (Not) Invisible to the Eye: Proust, Distraction, and Signs

In a well-known passage of *Le Temps retrouvé* (Time Regained), the protagonist of *À la recherche du temps perdu* has a crucial insight on his way to the Guermantes's matinée, when he trips on an uneven paving stone. The episode closely resembles the one narrated by Poincaré, who solved the problem that had troubled him for days when he rested his foot on the step of the omnibus.[1] Like Poincaré, Proust insists on the power of the involuntary and assigns a decisive role to distraction.

At first sight, the sudden insight gained at the Hôtel de Guermantes seems to retrace step by step the various stages of the invention process brought to light by Poincaré. After several unsuccessful attempts, the narrator has decided to abandon all literary ambitions: writing is not a pleasure for him but a task to which he dedicates himself with much effort and little enthusiasm. Discouraged, and now convinced of his total lack of talent, he accepted the Princess's invitation. Having no more time to gain, but only to lose, he can abandon himself without remorse to what, to him, are nothing but frivolous worldly pleasures (*divertissements*, Pascal would have said) compared to the happiness he had hoped to find in literature. Such happiness, however, he now knows for certain he cannot achieve—either because of his inability or perhaps because literature itself does not have the value that he had previously attributed to it. And yet it is precisely when he arrives at the Hôtel de Guermantes that the narrator, in a completely random and unexpected way, thanks to a series of external stimuli by which he allows himself to be distracted (the uneven pavement, the clink of a spoon against a plate, the stiffness of a starched napkin), has the revelation that directs him toward the path of literature. Although the joy of this revelation imposes itself in his mind with singular certainty, immediately dispelling all the doubts that preceded it, its meaning can only be fully understood with further effort.² In line with Poincaré's view, Proust too considers conscious work indispensable—provided, however, as Deleuze will point out, that it comes later, *a posteriori* and not *a priori*.³

Yet, despite appearances, the function of distraction is not exactly the same for Proust and Poincaré. According to the latter, as we have seen, distraction plays a decisive role at the moment of incubation when, shifting the attention of the conscious self elsewhere, it lets ideas swirl through the mind in every direction, like Epicurus's hooked atoms or gas molecules, until some of them spontaneously unite in a stable configuration. It is only in this way that unthinkable combinations of ideas can arise—combinations that the conscious mind would have been incapable of conceiving by itself. Unlike Cabanis and Chabaneix, Poincaré argues that unconscious creation does not consist of mere automatism and emphasizes both the role of "choice" and the importance of the subsequent conscious work. However, when it comes to defining the function of distraction in this process, he continues to think in terms of the associationist paradigm. For Proust, on the contrary, the importance of distraction does not so much have to do with the association of ideas but depends instead on the *structure of experience* which, as Benjamin has shown, in turn informs that of memory.⁴

This is why external stimuli, which for Poincaré do not perform any evocative function but simply occur in conjunction with the arrival of the insight, acquire a decisive importance in Proust's perspective. As in the passage of the madeleine dipped in tea, each of the apparently trivial and insignificant sensations distracting the protagonist during the Guermantes's matinée is unexpectedly able to bring back to life a past never expressly lived and apparently forgotten. And it is the possibility of this return that determines the literary conversion of the narrator.

Indeed, the way Proust describes the final illumination that the narrator had at the Hôtel de Guermantes has a "miraculous" quality to it that closely resembles Augustine's conversion.[5] It is in the moment of utmost discouragement and dejection, when all hope seems lost, that the decisive sign that we had sought for so long comes from where we least expect it:

> But it is sometimes just at the moment when we think that everything is lost that the intimation arrives which may save us; one has knocked at all the doors which lead nowhere, and then one stumbles without knowing it on the only door through which one can enter—which one might have sought in vain for a hundred years—and it opens of its own accord.
> (*Le Temps retrouvé*, Fr. 173, Eng. 254–5)

Proust does not hesitate to define the above sensations as many "visions," as the "signs" that restore the narrator's "faith in literature,"[6] suddenly dispelling all doubt and anxiety and making him feel extreme happiness, an almost mystical enjoyment, deeper and truer than the kind found in purely material pleasures.[7]

Of course the providential aspect of this experience, central to Augustine, is evoked by Proust only as an outer shell, as an illusion to which the mind wants to surrender itself: "it seemed as though the signs which were to bring me, on this day of all days, out of my disheartened state and restore to me my faith in literature, were thronging eagerly about me" (*Le Temps retrouvé*, Fr. 175, Eng. 258). The distraction produced by an external and apparently secondary stimulus, which in Augustine was part of a providential plan designed for human weakness in need of a sensory anchorage, becomes instead in Proust an essential condition inscribed in the very structure of experience. According to Proust, at the margins of every conscious experience we have, there is always a cloud of impressions to which we only pay distracted attention. If what we consciously experience—dictated by action and practical purposes, silently shaped by habit, and guided by intelligence—regularly makes us lose sight of what is essential, what we notice distractedly can give us access, albeit fleetingly, to the decisive and revealing aspects of every experience.

Proust is often considered the discoverer of involuntary memory, whose mechanism would be the basis of the entire novel *À la recherche du temps perdu*. In fact, Proust's great discovery has less to do with memory than with the power of distraction.[8] It is the latter that contains the key to understanding the coincidence between time lost and time regained. For Proust, it is only the time that we have lost—the time spent distractedly and without thinking about it, and therefore not fully lived and apparently forgotten—that can be properly regained and resurrected in its essence through memory.

This discovery, of which involuntary memory is but a corollary or a consequence, can be summed up as follows: what is essential, in every experience, is always what had first gone unnoticed and had only distractedly struck our attention, without entering into the full light of consciousness. What is essential goes unnoticed not—to quote the phrase of the *Little Prince*—because it is hidden and "invisible to the eye." On the contrary, it is clearly visible and perfectly accessible to the senses; only our perceptive habits, placed at the service of practical life and guided by intelligence, prevent us from paying attention to it. Proust shares with Bergson the idea that voluntary and conscious attention—aimed at action, directed to utility, and shaped by habit and language—regularly sidesteps what is essential.[9] It is, for example, because of habit, which teaches us to associate blond hair with blue eyes, that the narrator forgets about Gilberte's black eyes, a detail as distinctive as it is dissonant, and which instead had fleetingly struck him during their first meeting in Combray:

> [F]or a long time afterwards, whenever I thought of her, the memory of those bright eyes would at once present itself to me as a vivid azure, since she was blonde; so much so that, perhaps, if

her eyes had not been quite so black—which was what struck one most forcibly on first meeting her—I should not have been, as I was, especially enamored of their imagined blue.
(*Du côté de chez Swann*, Fr. 139, Eng. 198)

Common sense and education teach us to go beyond our first impressions. Psychology warns us against what is now called "unconscious bias," that is, the mechanism by which, when we judge things according to first impressions, we would be led to make choices based on irrational elements, such as prejudices, passions, and instinct, which affect all our decisions without us being aware of it. Yet, paradoxically, we should often trust precisely those details that we notice distractedly as our first impression and forget immediately afterward, when we make room for the abstract information that comes to us from habit and conscious experience. It is not uncommon that these first fugitive impressions, not yet embedded in a body of pre-constituted knowledge, detached from the rational picture that we will form later, are also those that resurface obliquely in our dreams or that will be confirmed later, with the progressive decomposition of the ideal image that conscious experience had established in their place. This was the case with Swann, for example, when the exhaustion of his love for Odette, who had been but "a long oblivion of the first impression that he had formed of her," gradually brought back to his mind, like a receding tide, the memory of the impressions that had struck him at first but he had forgotten immediately afterward as he began to frequent her: "To think that I've wasted years of my life, that I've longed to die, that I've experienced my greatest love for a woman, who didn't appeal to me, who wasn't even my type!" (*Du côté de chez Swann*, Fr. 375, Eng. 543).

Placed in the service of action, habit creates syntheses that cancel out the differences deemed less significant from a practical point of view. This is proven by the fact that, as Leopardi already noted, we often forget whether or not we have done the things that we do mechanically every day.[10] This is why what is essential and decisive is more easily revealed to those who are distracted and do not look at, or listen to, what everyone else is looking at or listening to. Like an inexperienced child who sees things for the first time, a distracted person is more struck by difference than similarities.[11] Their senses are as if disconnected from their practical function, as is the case with artists according to Bergson.[12] When painting a sunset, an artist is more interested in capturing the nuances of color rather than the approaching night—even at the risk of falling from a ladder, as happens to Hippolyte at the beginning of Balzac's *La bourse* (*The Purse*). In the same way, in a worldly conversation, distracted people are less attentive to what is being talked about than to the tone of voice or the way certain words are pronounced. Similarly, in social gesturing, they do not so much focus on the practical destination of the gestures they see, on the intention that expressly motivates them, or on their conventional and shared meaning. Rather, as is the case with the narrator of *La Recherche*, a distracted person cannot help but unwittingly pay attention to the unconscious micro-movements that accompany voluntary gestures—the sneer of the mouth, the excessive gravity of the voice,[13] or the exasperated zeal of a bow, such as the one made by Legrandin when introduced to the wife of a wealthy landowner:

> This rapid straightening-up caused a sort of tense muscular wave to ripple over Legrandin's rump, which I had not supposed to be so fleshy; I cannot say why, but this undulation of pure matter, this wholly carnal fluence devoid of spiritual significance, this wave lashed into a tempest by an obsequious alacrity of the basest sort, awoke my mind suddenly to the possibility of a Legrandin altogether different from the one whom we knew.
> (*Du côté de chez Swann*, Fr. 123, Eng. 174–5)

It is here—in the imperceptible gestures where voluntary effort is less intense, in the small inadvertent and seemingly insignificant movements—that a distracted person unintentionally grasps the signs that reveal a person's character, their dominant inclinations and passions. The involuntary movements that accompany voluntary actions without being determined by their purpose and intentions are indeed the gestures around which Balzac builds his *théorie de la démarche* (theory of walking) and which Schiller believed to reveal a person's mode of feeling. In those movements, an individual's interiority can be perfectly read in their exterior: "one can deduce from a person's words how they would like to be viewed, but what they really are must be guessed from the gestures accompanying their speech, in other words, from the uncontained movements."[14]

According to the art critic Giovanni Morelli, a connoisseur learns to recognize precisely these movements, when crystallized in a brushstroke, as the unmistakable hand of an artist, therefore establishing as a method the visual dissociation that is typical of states of distraction and allows one to break perceptual habits. Like a distracted person, a connoisseur does not pay attention to the main subjects of a painting but is captured by the negligible and less conspicuous details that normally go unnoticed and even escape the meticulous attention of imitators (the shape of an ear, the contour of a fingernail). Just as small unconscious gestures reveal our character more than any carefully studied and prepared attitude, so these secondary details, not culturally conditioned by any artistic movement and which not even the artist is aware of, contain the ineffable and unequivocal characteristics of their style.[15]

Just like the connoisseur, a caricaturist relies on the same "distracted" practice of looking when capturing the fossilization of certain involuntary gestures or movements in the expressiveness of facial forms and features. Caricatures manage to highlight, as Bergson put it, "the effort of a soul which is shaping matter,"[16] until any difference between depth and surface disappears. Once portrayed by a caricaturist even the original cannot help but show us the features that habit had prevented us from noticing until then.

Perhaps this is the unacknowledged reason for the irritation that we feel toward those who are distracted while we are talking: we know very well that if they are not listening to us it is because their attention has been captured by those secondary details where the truth comes out in spite of us. What these details reveal about us or others is often so inconsistent and dissonant compared to the conscious image of a certain person or situation that we rationally and consciously form through conversation and habitual acquaintance, that most of the time we end up doubting the truthfulness of those isolated and fleeting impressions in support of which we have nothing but the faint testimony of our senses.[17] This does not mean that the person who lets such imperceptible signs slip is deceitful or hypocritical when intentionally projecting a discordant self-image in words. As Proust's narrator notes:

> This was not to say that M. Legrandin was anything but sincere when he inveighed against snobs. He could not (from his own knowledge, at least) be aware that he himself was one, since it is only with the passions of others that we are ever really familiar, and what we come to find out about our own can only be learned from them.
>
> (*Du côté de chez Swann*, Fr. 127, Eng. 181)

Therefore, if words and voluntary movements can reveal something about others (or about ourselves) it is only if we observe them from a certain distance, as distracted people do: that is, if we do not pay attention to their intentional and explicit meaning, to their semantic and communicative value, but we read them obliquely, like a jealous lover would do with "a sudden rush of blood to the cheeks," "a sudden silence."[18]

Significantly, it is Françoise, the uneducated housekeeper, who teaches the narrator that the truth does not need to be told to manifest itself: "the truth has no need to be uttered to be made apparent, and [...] one may perhaps gather it with more certainty, without waiting for words and without taking any account of them, from countless outward signs."[19] This fact is well known to those who live in a foreign country without having mastered the language and therefore become more receptive to the details to which locals do not normally pay attention. "I, who for so many years had sought for the real life and thought of other people only in the direct statements with which they furnished me of their own free will, failing these had come to attach importance, on the contrary, only to the evidence that is not a rational and analytical expression of the truth" (*La Prisonnière*, Fr. 80, Eng. 109).

The kind of knowledge described here by Proust and based on the capacity of distraction seems to recall the cognitive method of psychoanalysis, which requires the use of what Freud called free-floating or evenly suspended attention (*gleichschwebende Aufmerksamkeit*). As he observes in one of the few texts he wrote for practicing analysts, "it must not be forgotten that the things one hears are for the most part things whose meaning is only recognized later on."[20] This is why the analyst must be wary of the traps set by voluntary or conscious attention: "as soon as anyone deliberately concentrates their attention to a certain degree, they begin to select from the material before them"; some material will be disregarded, and "in making this selection they will be following their expectations or inclinations." However, by following their expectations, analysts will never find anything but what they already know. Moreover, by following their inclinations, they risk falsifying what they perceive. On the contrary, free-floating attention, which "consists simply in not directing one's notice to anything in particular,"[21] can be captured by small and marginal details bearing latent and unexpressed content.[22]

As Freud explains, free-floating attention is, for the analyst, the necessary counterpart to the fundamental rule of psychoanalysis that is established for the patient. Just as the patient must communicate everything that occurs in their mind without criticism or selection and following the principle of "free associations," so the analyst "must put himself in a position to make use of everything he is told [...] without substituting a censorship of his own."[23] The analyst is required to remove "all conscious influences from his capacity to attend" and, in some ways, make use of what, with Proust, we could call involuntary memory:

> [The doctor] should simply listen, and not bother about whether he is keeping anything in mind. What is achieved in this manner will be sufficient for all requirements during the treatment. Those elements of the material which already form a connected context will be at the doctor's conscious disposal; the rest, as yet unconnected and in chaotic disorder, seems at first to be submerged, but rises readily into recollection as soon as the patient brings up something new to which it can be related.[24]

However, what Freud sees as *symptoms* are for Proust simple *signs* that call to be deciphered.[25] Even though they escape the conscious control of those who make them, in Proust spontaneous associations or involuntary movements revealing an otherwise unattainable truth, are not necessarily the expression of something *repressed* that emerges by forcing certain resistances. Nor is the unconscious speaking metaphorically or translating itself through them. What is telling, in Legrandin's bow, is not so much the corpulence of his backside (a characteristic that the narrator had not noticed until that moment), but rather the alacrity with which this character inadvertently performs the rapid movement that reveals it. As we will see, by reading a sign as a symptom, the risk is to make the same mistake as a jealous lover, whom Freud himself compares to the psychoanalyst.[26]

6. Involuntary Memory

Proust shares with Bergson the idea that memory preserves virtually all the past and that nothing of our experience is ever lost. Even what we have experienced in a distracted way, no less than what we have experienced consciously and deliberately, is preserved in memory, leading to the accumulation of remembrances of a completely different nature. While what has been part of our lived experience remains available to voluntary memory (the memory of intelligence) and can be retrieved at will if necessary, the unconscious or not fully lived side of any conscious experience—where the essential is hidden—can return unexpectedly only in moments of distraction. Indeed, there are memories that we may never know we have that yet are preserved. Their recovery does not depend on us but on the fortuitous encounter with certain objects that are for us the signs of a forgotten past ready to rise again. Not only may we never come across such objects, but we may not even recognize them if we do, driven as we are by practical needs and anaesthetizing habits, which make us pay attention only to what is useful.

This happens, for example, to Proust's narrator during a car trip around Balbec. From the car, he sees three trees that he seems to recognize, in a sort of déjà vu, but without having the time to fully grasp the reason behind this feeling: the trees "formed a pattern which I was not seeing for the first time. I could not succeed in reconstructing the place from which they had been as it were detached, but I felt that it had been familiar to me once."[1] Such memories resist evocation and lie out of our reach: for them to be resurrected, it is necessary to exercise the capacity for distraction, remaining alert and receptive to what is happening on the periphery of our conscious being, waiting for something that we cannot know in advance (and therefore actively and voluntarily seek), but only recognize when it comes to us. This capacity for distraction not only gives us access to the essential aspect of each experience but is also, at the same time, what enables its potential return.

As Deleuze observes, when the memory of Combray unexpectedly arises in the taste of a madeleine dipped in tea, it is not by simple associative means that it returns. Nor is the Combray that comes back through involuntary memory the same Combray that was the object of our conscious experience. What the distracting sensation of the madeleine involuntarily recalls is the essence of a past that had never been expressly experienced. This does not mean, however, that it is a "mythical" past, a time idealized and transfigured by the imagination. The idealization or mythification of the past is, if anything, a risk run by voluntary memory: continuing to go back over faces and situations, it often ends up altering the memory of them until we forget them altogether. Then we no longer know if what we remember was actually part of our experience or if it came from one of its many successive revisitations and representations, as happens for example with childhood photographs. Stendhal had already noticed this mechanism: thinking back to his legendary crossing of the Great St. Bernard Pass following the Napoleonic army, he realized how the image built later, resulting from prints, engravings, and the stories reported or heard afterward, eventually took the place of the original memory.[2]

If the past that returns through involuntary memory is a past that, as such, has never been present, it is because we experienced it distractedly. Unbeknownst to us, it inscribed itself in our memory, keeping itself intact and pure precisely because it had been forgotten.[3] That is why, if chance allows it to rise again, it can give us back the essence of things, people, or situations that we believed to have fallen into oblivion. According to Proust, only what has not been consciously experienced is intact in memory, preserved in the seemingly more insignificant details we recorded without paying attention to them. Thus, the hostile roughness of a hotel towel preserves the essence of the narrator's summer stays in Balbec, the sound of a hammer against the wheel of a stationary train crystallizes the memory of a row of trees seen from the window many years before, and the uneven pavement of St. Mark's Square encapsulates the sensory idea of Venice.

In their insignificance, all these impressions, to which the narrator had only paid attention distractedly and which he had never thought about again, have preserved something of his past that can now be brought back to life by similar sensations, such as the stiffness of a starched napkin, the sound of a spoon bumping against a plate, or the uneven pavement in the courtyard of the Hôtel de Guermantes. This past, inaccessible to intelligence and the will, can only rise again if we let ourselves be distracted by a present sensation that unexpectedly resonates with that of the past. So, taking advantage of this brief moment of distraction of the conscious self, which leaves the senses free from the organization imposed on them by the demands of practical life, the past resurrects so suddenly that it determines an even more powerful distraction, which tears us away from the present and, so to speak, turns us into somnambulists.

7. The Spider and the Connoisseur: On Art, Literary Vocation, and Jealousy

This is why, according to Proust, truth or essence—the subject of art—has a privileged relationship with memory and requires the exercise of distraction. It is thanks to the latter, which implies a different form of attention and receptivity, that alongside every conscious and expressly lived experience we can build a reserve of unlived experiences in which the past is preserved intact in our memory, regardless of whether we become aware of it or not. And it is only by exercising the capacity for distraction, remaining receptive to seemingly secondary external stimuli, that we ensure that this past can be resurrected. What an artist must do, therefore, is to make use of their capacity for distraction, the only one through which they can access what is *essential*, in the double sense of crucial and relating to the essence of things. It is this discovery that produces in the narrator a true literary conversion.

Swann, a refined art connoisseur and collector, had already put him on the right track. As a connoisseur, Swann knows that the unmistakable style of an artist, for example a painter, should not be sought in the main subjects of their work but can be recognized by the seemingly negligible details where voluntary effort is less intense. Swann, however, had ended up putting his talent as a connoisseur—the same talent that had once nurtured his studies and animated his passion for history and for deciphering texts and works of art—entirely at the service of his jealous love for Odette, in a vain attempt to discover the truths (the betrayals) that her gestures and lies obliquely revealed to him:

> [T]he curiosity which he now felt stirring inside him with regard to the smallest details of a woman's daily life, was the same thirst for knowledge with which he had once studied history. And all manner of actions from which hitherto he would have recoiled in shame, such as spying, tonight, outside a window, tomorrow perhaps, for all he knew, putting adroitly provocative questions to casual witnesses, bribing servants, listening at doors, seemed to him now to be precisely on a level with the deciphering of manuscripts, the weighing of evidence, the interpretation of old monuments.
> (*Du côté de chez Swann*, Fr. 269–70, Eng. 389)

Adapting this method of investigation to the search for the infidelities that his mistress conceals from him, the greatest risk, for Swann, is not so much that of becoming ridiculous. His sense of dignity is in fact infinitely superseded by his desire to know the truth, which gives him unparalleled pleasure. The real danger, which Swann is not even aware of, is losing sight of the essential aspect that guides this method of knowledge and guarantees its truthfulness. That is, the truth is not to be discovered, but is betrayed, and all the signs that we strive to decipher are true only if they come to us when we are not looking for them—only if we notice them distractedly, before intelligence intervenes. In fact, intelligence can only mislead us and steer us on the wrong track if it takes over at the beginning rather than at the end. It is no coincidence that Swann confuses Odette's window with another one, the night in which, determined to discover the truth, he goes to his lover's house to spy on her through the shutters.[1]

As we have seen, the narrator, who only after Albertine's death will be able to free himself from this misunderstanding induced by jealousy, fully understands the cognitive scope of distraction only at the end of the novel. The truth, the essence, is something we can only come across: something that can only chance upon us from the outside. The best an artist can do is wait patiently, like a spider listening to the smallest vibrations of its web.[2] Like a spider, a writer is blind—or rather, they pay no attention to what everyone else is looking at, because they know that there is really nothing to see there. The writer, like the spider, waits for something they do not know, but can only recognize when it occurs. That is why the only form of attention the writer trusts is the involuntary kind, the kind of attention typical of moments of distraction, when apparently nothing is happening and the spider is curled up on itself in a kind of sleep or catalepsy. The capacity for distraction, which a writer must keep alert by becoming receptive, on the periphery of their conscious being, to the small perceptions that most often go unnoticed, is like the web that a spider unfolds around itself, taking it from within. This is a kind of attention that, to quote Simone Weil, we cannot *want* but only *desire*.[3]

Proust teaches us that art is essentially about distraction. But not in the obvious and banal sense that art allows us to escape from the world or from reality. On the contrary, art requires and promotes another way of looking at the world and at reality: a way that is made possible by distraction as a particular mode of attention that is constitutively different from voluntary and conscious attention and that, as such, gives us access to a different form of experience and memory. For Proust it is always distractedly—unwittingly—that we come across the truth. It is always by letting ourselves be distracted by what appears to be of no importance (by perceptions that fall on the side of conscious experience and suspend perceptive habits for a moment) that we make the decisive discoveries which nourish art and literature. When Elstir paints the sea with earthy qualities and the land with marine characteristics, he depicts not what he *knows* but what he distractedly *sees*, remaining faithful to "the optical illusions of which our first sight of things is composed."[4] The artist thus foregoes the explanations proposed by abstract intelligence, which immediately rushes to tell us that no, of course what we are looking at cannot be the sea (or vice versa), and makes us forget the fugitive impression that had captured the essence common to both.

Thanks to the consolidation of this discovery, the protagonist becomes able to correct the other mistake Swann had made. The latter had ended up using art the other way around: not to grasp what is essential by exercising the capacity for distraction, but to fix his attention (his love) on a particular individual. Instead of seeing the resemblance between Odette and Botticelli's Zipporah as proof of an essence that, captured by the painter, he casually finds in the face of his beloved, Swann makes this resemblance a reason to consciously and rationally motivate his love for a woman who is not really his type. If Swann's interest in the history of art finds something of the passion of yesteryear, it is only to the extent that it is guided and illuminated by the memory of Odette, evoked by Renaissance paintings.[5]

Like an aesthete, Swann turns art into a subjective form of compensation and uses it to embellish and legitimize the already given fabric of his daily experience.[6] Swann knows well that the task of art is to reject clichés, breaking down ordinary perception and allowing us to see what we consciously pay no attention to: it is precisely because they ignore the true function of art that Cottard and his wife are simply unable to understand the beauty of the Vinteuil sonata or Biche's portraits, each of which they see as nothing more than a jumble of notes or colors where they recognize nothing of the shapes to which they are accustomed.[7] And yet Swann himself ends up reducing art to clichés, when he begins to limit its enjoyment to the satisfaction of finding Odette's traits in it. In this way, Swann loses sight of the fact that the function of art is to break the patterns imposed by ordinary perception, so as to allow us to grasp the essence that normally goes unnoticed and which we can only experience distractedly.[8]

8. "The Entire History of You"

Those familiar with the TV show *Black Mirror* will remember an episode from the first season, entitled "The Entire History of You," which presents an idea of experience and memory only apparently similar to Proust's. The technological advancement of a not-too-distant future allows human beings to implant a small device (called "grain") under the skin, behind the ear lobe, which allows them to record every single experience in a faithful and detailed way. Thanks to this artificial enhancement of individual memory, everyone has at their disposal a potentially infinite reserve of memories to consult and analyze at will or as needed. The benefit of such a device is obvious. In addition to perfecting security checks (at the airport, together with luggage, the security staff also inspect the recent memories of passengers waiting to board), it makes our past always at hand, ready to provide all the evidence or answers we are looking for.

Whenever we are in doubt about something, all we have to do is rewind the recording stored in the "grain" to the desired point, send it forward in slow motion, and then zoom in on the details involved, artificially shifting the focus of our attention to what had gone unnoticed at first until we unravel and make all the perceptions enveloped in each experience clear and distinct. Thus, for example, after a job interview, the protagonist can guess the outcome even before being told, simply by analyzing the mental recording of the meeting and zooming in on the minute but unequivocal signs that appear in the interviewers' faces, gestures, or words. Similarly, much like the jealous lover Proust talks about, the protagonist of the episode can use all the resources of memory and intelligence to discover the secret that his girlfriend does not want to reveal to him: it is enough for him to analyze retrospectively the micro-movements entangled in her gestures and words. The truth, sooner or later, will come out in the texture of some freeze frame, finally confirming his doubts and giving him a real "pleasure of intelligence," quite similar to the one Swann felt in front of the illuminated window: "When you suspect something, it's always better when it turns out to be true."

Essentially, thanks to this recording device, the secondary details, which we initially detect only distractedly, are no longer signs to interpret and decipher, as in Proust, but become simple images to analyze and unravel, as in a sort of cinematic optical unconscious. But this is not the only difference. For Proust, the past that is preserved in our memory can reveal the essence or truth of things and situations only if it resurfaces involuntarily, thanks to a chance encounter. In other words, for Proust, the decisive details, which initially escaped conscious attention, are inaccessible to the zoom of voluntary memory and intelligence, which always and inevitably give us a false image of the past. These signs are only true if we come across them in a distracted way, unintentionally, because only in this way can we play ahead of our intelligence, which, when guiding us (rather than intervening later), always leads us astray. Voluntarily solicited and placed in the service of intelligence, as in the *Black Mirror* episode, memory can only condemn to failure the search for truth. The truth is not to be discovered by goodwill but is betrayed by involuntary signs.

By poking through memory under the guidance of intelligence and the will, the jealous lover can, like the protagonist of the episode, form theories that may even be correct from a logical point of view, but that are unlikely to be true.[1] In the Hegelian mind of the jealous lover, not only is everything that is real necessarily rational, but also everything that is rational is real. As happens to Swann in front of what he believes to be Odette's window, the jealous person regularly falls into error every time they use intelligence not *a posteriori* but *a priori*. They will always end up being fooled by the wrong signs when, striving to remember, they let themselves be led by intelligence and voluntary memory. The decisive and revealing signs are likely to reveal themselves only when the jealous lover stops looking for them, in a moment of distraction while busy doing something else. But then, paradoxically, those signs will no longer be of any use because if the lover has stopped looking for them it means that their love has long since ended.

Memories capable of giving us what is essential, which is always found in what had previously gone unnoticed, cannot be recalled by us. They are not contained in memory as a series of frames which we can access and zoom into countless times. And perhaps this is also their saving grace, if you like. If the past could be fathomed and analyzed at will and be docile to the solicitations of voluntary memory, we would probably be trapped in it. Only apparently close to the one expressed by Proust, an idea of experience and memory such as the one depicted in *Black Mirror* actually misses its essential aspect because it loses sight of the decisive difference that exists between the two levels of experience (conscious and distracted) and the two types of memory that derive from it. By making distraction and oblivion impossible, a device like a "grain" would prevent us from grasping and remembering what is essential.

Part Three

Rêverie

Avant-propos

What are we thinking about when we are distracted? Usually, we tell ourselves that we are not thinking about anything at all. Or at least, that's what we say when someone brings us back to reality after a moment of absent-mindedness and asks us what we were thinking about. Being distracted when in the company of other people is generally considered disrespectful.[1] In such cases we often make fools of ourselves by doing or saying things out of context, as happens to La Bruyère's Ménalque, a parody of the absent-minded person.[2] On top of that, distraction almost always betrays a clear lack of interest in those present: for Diderot, it "lets them know very clearly that what is happening in our minds is far more interesting to us than what they are saying."[3] By stating that we were not thinking about anything at all, we feel we are excusing, at least in part, our absent-mindedness.

However, we know very well that this is not quite the case. Coming back to ourselves after a moment of distraction, we are often engaged in thoughts whose origin we do not really know and which seem to have no relation to the present situation. While we are sitting at dinner with some guests talking about buying a new car, we find ourselves unwittingly thinking back to the careless glance we exchanged with a stranger while leaving the cinema. These evanescent thoughts, which tend to disappear after a few moments like waking dreams, are the elusive content of distraction—the things we think about when we are distracted. They correspond to that state of mind we call *rêverie* (reverie).

1. Dreams, Reveries, Fantasies

As the word itself suggests, "reverie" is a kind of dream (*rêve*) that we have with our eyes open. Like the French verb *rêver* (to dream), the term "reverie" is said to derive from the Latin *exvagus*, composed of *ex* (outside) and *vagus* (vagabonding, wandering about). Etymologically close to the term "extravagant" (from *extravagante*), reverie would therefore contain, at least originally, the idea of wandering and vagabondage.[1]

Locke was one of the first to give a rigorous definition of this term. For him, reverie was not absence of thought but rather a particular mode of thinking, similar to dreaming and ecstasy, where ideas follow each other spontaneously and without any precise order:

> When ideas float in our mind, without any reflection or regard of the understanding, it is that, which the French call *resvery*; our language has scarce a name for it [...]. And dreaming itself is the having of Ideas [...] in the mind, not suggested by any external objects, or known occasion; nor under any choice or conduct of the understanding at all. And whether that, which we call *extasy* be not dreaming with the eyes open, I leave to be examined.
>
> (*Essay*, II, ch. 19, § 1)

As Locke points out, the French term *rêverie* is one of those words for which there is no appropriate translation in English: hence the calque "reverie." In fact, if the word "daydream," attested as a noun since the mid-seventeenth century, fails to express the essentially rhapsodic and wandering aspect of this mental attitude (the idea of thoughts roaming or vagabonding in the mind), on the other hand, the expression "mind-wandering," introduced in the nineteenth century, loses the fundamental link with dreaming.[2]

The Italian term *fantasticheria* (the act of fantasizing about something) does not seem to offer an adequate translation either. If the boundaries between these two mental states are very thin and often tend to blur, *rêverie* and *fantasticheria* do not indicate exactly the same phenomenon. A *fantasticheria* does not make us lose sight of the contours of reality, nor does it ever question the authority of the senses or of the external world. However bizarre and far-fetched it may be, a *fantasticheria* is still guarded by consciousness and guided by the will: we can fantasize about whatever we want (getting a promotion at work, winning the lottery, going on vacation) or build castles in the air that trace the contours of our desires, consciously allowing our thoughts to linger on pleasant images.[3] On the contrary, it is always without realizing it that we fall into reverie and it is often abruptly that we awaken from it—like when a burning smell, suddenly claiming our attention, brings us back to a present from which we had unwisely absented ourselves.

Like a dream, reverie is spontaneous and makes us lose track of space and time. Just as a few seconds in a dream can cover, in the mind, the arc of an entire day, so (as Diderot observes) "distraction is an absence [...] whose duration we are almost never aware of." There is only one way to measure how long it lasted: "it consists in being able to relate its beginning and end to two different moments of a continuous action whose duration we know from experience."[4] For instance, the name of a metro stop can give us a vague idea of how long we have been lost in our thoughts, based on how far away the station is from where we were supposed to get off. If we had no way of referring to something external (the time marked by the clock, a change in light, the soreness of a limb), it would be practically impossible to realize how much time has actually passed while we were caught in our reverie.[5]

Similar to a dream, a reverie always extends beyond our intentions and, once interrupted, it is impossible to pick up its thread. Dream and reverie are not based on imagination or fantasy in the modern sense—that is, on the ability to make-believe, to bring about (to paraphrase Coleridge) a willing and temporary suspension of disbelief, the same suspension that allows children to play cops and robbers in the living room or adults to read a novel or watch a movie. In situations like these, Leopardi rightly observes, "the intellect, amidst the delirium of the imagination, is all the while aware that it is delirious."[6] Instead, dream and reverie are based on the capacity for distraction (from the Latin *distrahere*, to separate, to detach from). It is precisely this capacity that, by dulling our senses for a moment, allows us to absent ourselves from the present and from the shared world. In this sense, as Bergson would observe, "the dream-self is a distracted self."[7]

Unlike what happens during wakefulness, when we dream or indulge in some reverie, as Locke had already pointed out, the mind is *distracted*, "retired as it were from the senses, and out of the reach of those motions made on the organs of sense, which at other times produce very vivid and sensible ideas" (*Essay*, II, ch. 19, § 4). Someone who is deeply asleep can spend a whole stormy night without noticing the lightning and thunder. Likewise, those who are lost in their thoughts cease for a moment to perceive what is happening around them and see nothing but the succession of ideas taking place in their reverie. The balance that normally reigns between sensations and images is broken in favor of the latter and, as Taine would observe, sensations weaken as images grow stronger.[8]

In a way, we can think of reverie as the mirror image of the sensation of déjà vu: if in déjà vu the object of perception seems to cross over into the imagination and to double itself in a memory, in reverie it is instead what we imagine that tends to erase what we perceive.[9] In its hallucinatory character, reverie reveals itself, as we shall see, to be dangerously closer to madness than to fantasy.

2. Reverie and Childhood: On Sand, Proust, and Flaubert

Fantasy—or make-believe—is an activity of the mind that, according to Piaget,[1] would allow children to become adults; it is through play that children supposedly engage in a process of progressive adaptation and assimilation of their future identities. Reverie, on the contrary, is a mental state that makes us *regress* to childhood, a time when the boundaries of things, as well as those of our personality, were still fluid and undecided.[2]

Few have been able to capture the reveries of childhood as well as George Sand.[3] What she depicts are not so much reveries *about* childhood but rather, more radically, reveries we engaged in as children—those in which we lost ourselves in the contemplation of a tapestry, the swirling of dust in a sunbeam, or the reflections of fire on the fire screen:

> I was seated at my mother's feet, in front of the fire, and between me and the hearth stood an old four-legged screen lined with green taffeta. I could see a little of the fire through the worn taffeta; it produced little stars on the fabric, whose glow I could augment by squinting. Then, little by little, I lost the thread of the sentences my mother was reading; her voice cast me into a state of mental drowsiness that made it impossible to pursue one thought. Images took shape before my eyes and settled on the green fire screen. There were forests, meadows, rivers, cities of strange and gigantic

architecture of the kind I still often see in my dreams; enchanted palaces with gardens the likes of which do not exist, with thousands of blue and gold and crimson birds that hovered above the flowers and could be caught as easily as one might pluck a rose.[4]

Rarely, as adults, can we relive something that even remotely approaches the ecstatic rapture of childhood reverie. And this is not only because childhood is practically the only age of life in which one can indulge in distraction without scruples or guilt. Between reverie and childhood there is an intrinsic and primordial link, even more decisive and profound than the one by which we nostalgically idealize childhood as the age of play and fantasy. What characterizes childhood reveries is an immediate adhesion to the sensory world, to the *present moment* of sensation. In them, all awareness of one's individuality fades away and the event or situation—in this case, reading in front of the fire—dissolves into a confused game of sensations and images in which objects lose their meaning as well as any practical use.

But it is not only the instrumental function of things (what Heidegger called *Zuhandenheit*)[5] that is lost. Untied from the web of meanings that we normally establish around them and from the corresponding sensory organization, the elements of perception become available for new configurations or imaginative transfigurations. A perfectly ordered space, where objects are well arranged and separated from each other, is replaced by an indeterminate space where things are mixed and deformed, and their contours merge together. In cases like these, it seems that reverie, even more than tearing us away from the present, makes us adhere more strongly to it, deepening and amplifying perception in a sort of hallucinatory state. Thus, in the passage above, the reflections of the fire on the fire screen, filtered through half-closed eyes, give life to a flow of unreal figures that transform into one another, while the reading voice crumbles into a meaningless chant that is still heard without being listened to.

A very similar experience is described by Proust at the beginning of his novel *À la recherche du temps perdu*. While in church with his parents to celebrate the "Month of Mary," the narrator is distracted by the position and scent of the hawthorns adorning the altar. Breaking down the mystical solemnity of the religious rite into its sensory elements, the young protagonist indulges in the purely sensual contemplation of these sacred flowers: the careless grace of their lowered corolla is transfigured, in his reverie, into the "swift and thoughtless movement of the head, with a provocative glance from her contracted pupils, by a young girl in white, insouciant and vivacious," while the powerful bittersweet fragrance of almonds spread by the hawthorns around them, in spite of their modest and silent demeanor, transforms the altar into a luxuriant hedge, visited by "living antennae" and quivering with the vibration of intense spring life.[6]

It is difficult not to think of another episode of reverie that also dissolves the composed organization of a liturgical event. Its protagonist is young Emma, the future Madame Bovary, who, in the warm atmosphere of the convent, lasciviously indulges during mass in "a mystical languor by the scents on the altar, the coolness of the holy-water stoups, and the radiance of the candles." Instead of paying attention to the service, "she would study, in her missal, the pious illustrations with their sky-blue borders" and found particular delight in "the sick lamb, the Sacred Heart pierced by sharp arrows, and poor Jesus, stumbling under the burden of his cross. She attempted, as a mortification, to go a whole day without eating."[7]

Perhaps even more radically than what we have seen in George Sand and Proust, in Flaubert the young protagonist's reverie disperses the ongoing event into a stream of sensations and images that remain unconnected, devoid of any further sense or meaning. In fact, no one better than Flaubert seems to have captured, in Gérard Genette's words, this "escape of meaning into the indefinite trembling of things" so characteristic of the reveries of childhood. In the abundance of gratuitous and insignificant details that seem to overload the mental ramblings of his characters, in that excess of material presence that seems to undermine the verisimilitude of an experience that is in principle subjective and that, as such, would have required "vague, diffuse, elusive evocations,"[8] Flaubert actually captured the most extreme aspect of reverie. In its ecstatic nature, reverie implies precisely a mode of being *outside* oneself *in* things, so close to them as to lose oneself in their simple materiality.

According to Flaubert, this ecstatic and fusional rapture in the most insignificant things is the object of St. Anthony's pantheistic temptation:

> Often, apropos of nothing, a drop of water, a shell, a hair, you stopped dead, your eyes staring, your heart open.
> The object you contemplated seemed to encroach on you, the closer you leant toward it, and ties were established; you hugged each other tight, you touched each other by means of subtle, innumerable grips [*adhérences*]; then, by dint of looking, you could no longer see; while listening, you could no longer hear anything, and your own soul ended up losing the notion of its own particularity.[9]

As it appears from the words addressed to him by the Spinozistic devil, the temptation besieging the saint seems to be nothing more than a desire to regress toward a state that we have often experienced in the empty afternoons of our childhood, when we would let the most trivial objects (the circle left on the table by a glass, the folds of a fabric, the written characters of a page that we were reading) linger distractedly in our gaze for an unspecified time. As Flaubert himself confides in a letter to Louise Colet, "sometimes by dint of looking at a pebble, an animal, a picture, I have felt myself enter into them."[10] This is how Thomas De Quincey imagined the last days of Immanuel

Kant: "during this state of repose, he took his station winter and summer by the stove, looking through the window at the old tower of Löbenicht; not that he could be said properly to see it, but the tower rested upon his eyes as distant music on the ear—obscurely, or but half revealed to the consciousness."[11]

3. Travel, Motion, Solitude: Rousseau and the Pleasures of Reverie

If Locke gave a content to distraction, identifying reverie not as an absence of thought but as a particular way of thinking, Rousseau, on the other hand, is the one who described its possible forms and manifestations. As suggested by the very title of the journal in which he jotted down the mental ramblings that accompanied his walks, *Les Rêveries du promeneur solitaire* (The Reveries of the Solitary Walker), reverie seems to require two fundamental conditions: movement and solitude.

Often considered as an imaginary journey that does not imply any physical displacement, in fact, reverie is not necessarily associated with stillness. As Rousseau had already observed in *Les Confessions*, there is an essential link between thinking and walking: more precisely, between motion and that freer and more vital form of thinking that we experience in moments of reverie, when ideas seem to flow spontaneously from one another, without purpose or precise order, and thinking itself ceases to be a laborious and tiring activity. In Rousseau's words:

> Never have I thought so much, existed so much, lived so much, been myself so much, if I dare to speak this way, as in these travels I have made alone and on foot. Walking has something that animates and enlivens my ideas: I almost cannot think when I stay in place; my body must be in motion to set my mind in motion.[1]

The fact is that movement spontaneously sets thought in motion, producing a series of modifications in the mind that prevent it from becoming fixed. Ideas then follow one another effortlessly, suggested by external stimuli that freely resonate with inner images.

That is why—as Leopardi would specify by adapting Rousseau's motif in a direction that already points to Proust—one of the main pleasures of a journey consists precisely in the involuntary memory that motion itself triggers in the mind of the traveler: "Those who have traveled much [...] observe that for them one of the causes of pleasure, when traveling, is that, having seen many places, the ones which they happen to go through from time to time easily recall others to mind that they have seen before, and that this reminiscence, in and of itself, is a delight" (*Zibaldone*, 4471). By spontaneously recalling the memory of things and people encountered in the past, travel puts the mind in a state of continuous reverie that thickens and doubles the fabric of perceptual experience. The mental state of the traveler then comes very close to that of people with a strong imagination. Indeed,

> to a sensitive and imaginative man, who lives [...] continually feeling and imagining, the world and its objects are in a certain respect double. With his eyes he will see a tower, a landscape; with his ears he will hear the sound of a bell; and at the same time with his imagination he will see another tower, another landscape, he will hear another sound. The whole beauty and pleasure of things lies in this second kinds of objects.
>
> (*Zibaldone*, 4418)

The journeys that nourished Rousseau's reveries were preferably made on foot, sometimes crossing the woods and mountains between France, Switzerland, and Italy, sometimes wandering aimlessly in the countryside.[2] In Leopardi's day, journeys were still made, when not on foot, mainly by carriage.[3] However, according to Proust, it is even easier to fall into similar states of reverie when contemplating the images that flow past the window of an automobile or a train in motion. Only fleetingly glimpsed and free from the wear and tear of habit, places, faces, and names of towns or cities are able to evoke unknown and hitherto unthinkable life possibilities. And, even more than traveling by car, which allows the traveler to stop at will, journeying by train is the best way, according to Proust, to feed our reverie, preserving the mysterious charm that places and names have in our imagination. As children, the main pleasure of imagination consisted in that fact that it "bore us from the place in which we were living right to the very heart of a place we longed to see, in a single sweep which seemed miraculous to us not so much because it covered a certain distance as because it united two distinct individualities of the world, took us from one name to another name." Likewise, the pleasure of traveling by train (and even more so, we might add, by plane) consists precisely in "making the difference between departure and arrival not as imperceptible but as intense as possible, so that we are conscious of it in its totality, intact, as it existed in our mind."[4]

However, as Rousseau himself experienced during his confinement on the Island of Saint-Pierre in the middle of Lake Bienne, the movement suitable for reverie can be either *subjective* or *objective*—that is, it can be not only the motion of the subject but also of the objects around them. If a journey or a walk can arouse reverie, this state of mind can also be triggered by particular visual or sonorous sensations, such as the regular motion of ripples on the surface of a lake or the lapping of water, with its alternating and continuous noise: "without any movement life is mere lethargy. If the movement is irregular or too violent it arouses us from our dreams; recalling us to an awareness of the surrounding objects, it destroys the charm of reverie."[5] As Bergson would later explain, uniform, cadenced movements lull the mind into a kind of hypnosis similar to that produced by particular musical rhythm or by the symmetry of artistic forms: by swinging the attention between two fixed points, they "put to sleep the active or rather resistant powers of our personality,"[6] so that the self, nearly losing the perception of time and of itself, can surrender to a stream of indistinct thoughts that follow one another without the active participation of the mind.

As Rousseau also notes, in the absence of external movement, "the movement which does not come from outside us arises within us." In this case it is the imagination that spontaneously generates pleasant and whimsical thoughts that, without stirring the bottom of the soul, barely ripple the surface, as the wind does when it brushes against the expanse of a lake. This type of reverie has an obvious benefit: given the right mental disposition, it "can be enjoyed anywhere where one is undisturbed." So much so that—as Rousseau paradoxically clarifies— "I have often thought that in the Bastille, and even in a dungeon with not a single object to rest my eyes on, I could still have dreamed pleasantly."[7]

As we saw in Part One, Pascal was convinced that a man left alone in a room, even with enough goods to live comfortably, would inevitably be assailed by boredom and despair, so incapable are we of enduring the sight of ourselves (hence the pressing need for *divertissement*). On the contrary, Rousseau sees this situation, reduced to its minimum terms, as the ideal condition for rediscovering the supreme pleasure of distraction and reverie. This pleasure implies a different relationship with time, one that is inoperative and unproductive.[8] This is the secret that, in Leopardi's famous dialogue staged in the hospital of Sant'Anna, the *genio familiare* (familial spirit) would reveal to the imprisoned Torquato Tasso: solitude in reality "almost performs the same function as youth; it certainly rejuvenates one's spirit, strengthens and gives new vigor to the power of the imagination," leading us even to forget the unpleasantness of boredom.[9]

In his *Voyage autour de ma chambre* (Voyage around My Room), Xavier de Maistre—younger brother of the more famous and austere Joseph—staged the hilarious mental ramblings of a man who, following a duel, is forced to spend forty-two days locked in his room. Here he refines the subtle art of being pleasantly distracted by the most insignificant things (the bubbling of water in the coffee pot, the subdued noise of breakfast preparations, or the chirping of birds) to the point that, shortly before regaining his freedom, he mockingly insinuates the suspicion that perhaps ordinary life is the real imprisonment:

> So today is the day of my freedom, or rather the day that I shall put my shackles back on. The yoke of worldly matters will weigh heavy on me once again; I shall no longer take a single step that is not measured by decorum and duty.—If only some capricious goddess would make me forget both, so that I could escape this new and dangerous captivity! Why did they not let me finish my voyage! Was it really to punish me that they confined me to my room?[10]

Perhaps Stendhal alludes to the same paradox in the final part of *Le Rouge et le Noir* (The Red and the Black). Locked up in the Besançon prison, Julien Sorel finally achieves a happiness that he had unsuccessfully hoped to obtain by means of much struggle: the pure and disinterested pleasure of reverie, whose subversive scope consists not so much in *overturning* but rather in *suspending* the social order and its organization of time, ceasing to take part in the game of their intrigues and duties. This pleasure is no different from the one hinted at by Rousseau, Leopardi, and Xavier de Maistre: a pleasure that is all too often forgotten and which, as Jacques Rancière has observed in commenting on these pages by Stendhal, is nothing more than the enjoyment of "the quality of sensible experience that one reaches when one stops calculating, wanting, and waiting, as soon as one resolves to do nothing."[11]

Except for exceptional circumstances, from this perspective, no confinement or physical imprisonment could prevent one from enjoying the supreme and clandestine pleasure of reverie. This is a clandestine pleasure because it is enjoyed in defiance of those who imprison or discipline the body, and indeed it is paradoxically discovered precisely thanks to their persecution. This is why, as Rousseau points out, reverie is also a *stable* pleasure that cannot be taken away from us—a pleasure sheltered not only from the blows of fortune but also from the envy and jealousy of other people.[12] Indeed, in the words of Leopardi, who would ever want to "make love by looking through a telescope" (*fare all'amore col telescopio*)?[13] Furthermore, it is a pleasure that is free of charge, as Xavier de Maistre jokingly points out, mocking the narrow-minded and self-interested bourgeois mentality, for which such a pleasure is simply incomprehensible:

> I could begin the praise of my voyage by saying that it cost me nothing. This point merits some attention. It will, at first, be extolled and celebrated by people of middling circumstances; yet there is another class of people with whom it is even more certain to enjoy great success, for the same reason, that it costs nothing. And who would these people be? Need you even ask? The rich, of course.
>
> (*Voyage*, ch. 2, p. 42; Eng. trans. p. 19)

After all, according to Rousseau, solitude proves to be no less indispensable to reverie than movement. By making us forget our dependence on things and on the world, it produces a healthy self-oblivion that spurs the course of our thoughts as well as our steps. This is when our ideas spring up in waves:

> [A]ll this disengages my soul, gives me a greater audacity in thinking, throws me in some manner into the immensity of beings in order to combine them, choose them, appropriate them at my whim without effort and without fear. I dispose of all nature as its master; wandering from object to object my heart unites, identifies

with the ones that gratify it, surrounds itself with charming images, makes itself drunk with delightful feelings.[14]

However—and this is an aspect that escaped Rousseau's phenomenology—the solitude suitable for reverie is not only that which is experienced away from society, be it in a rural retreat, in the bedroom, or in an isolation cell. There is an urban dimension to the pleasure of reverie that Rousseau was reluctant to admit. For the *flâneur*, it is the urban space that recreates the conditions favorable to the experience of imaginative solitude. While for Rousseau any human trace in what he believed to be an isolated refuge was enough to spoil the pleasure of reverie,[15] Baudelaire, on the contrary, would speak of the art of enjoying a crowd (*jouir de la foule*):

> It is not given to every man to take a bath of multitude; enjoying a crowd is an art; and only he can relish a debauch of vitality [*ribote de vitalité*] at the expense of the human species, on whom, in his cradle, a fairy has bestowed the love of masks and masquerading, the hatred of home, and the passion for wandering.
>
> Multitude, solitude: identical terms, and interchangeable by the active and fertile poet. The man who is unable to people his solitude is equally unable to be alone in a bustling crowd.[16]

4. Distraction and Automatism: *le moi d'habitude* and *le moi de réflexion*

In moments of reverie, when our eyes seem to look without seeing and our ears to hear without listening, we enter a state of semi-sensory suspension very close to somnambulism. It is not uncommon for our body mechanically to continue unperturbed with its daily chores, such as toasting bread, making coffee, or unerringly guiding our steps to work.

In moments like these we tangibly experience the coexistence of two distinct selves, which Condillac called *le moi de réflexion* (the self of reflection) and *le moi d'habitude* (the self of habit).[1] It is *le moi d'habitude* that allows a mathematician to walk across the whole city of Paris, turning without fail at every street corner and carefully dodging all obstacles, while the other self (*le moi de réflexion*) ponders a geometry problem, mentally reviews a lesson, or indulges in a tortuous course of thought. By dispensing us from the need to pay conscious attention to everyday actions, *le moi d'habitude* frees up mental space for us to think about something else. In this sense, distraction is a luxury we allow ourselves when we have achieved perfect automatism in a given operation. Then we can afford to let our minds wander, no longer needing to think constantly about what we are doing. A perfectly automated animate body—let's say a conscious robot of the kind imagined by Samuel Butler in *Erewhon or Over the Range*—would probably be in a state of continuous reverie, always thinking of something else.

The automatism of habit certainly produces distraction: while it improves the capacity to act, at the same time it removes the capacity to feel and be aware of what we are doing. This phenomenon has been observed and studied by the main theorists of habit, from Maine de Biran to Ravaisson, and further explored by William James.[2] However, it seems that most of the time this is only a relative distraction. If on the one hand a minimum degree of bodily attention persists even in movements that have become automatic, enabling corrections and adjustments of which we are not entirely aware, on the other hand conscious attention, freed from the need to attend to these movements, can be occupied by other processes.

It is precisely the power of habit that allows a musician to flawlessly complete the performance of a piece while their mind has drifted elsewhere. Indeed, as Samuel Butler observes, it is precisely this healthy absence or distraction of *le moi de réflexion* that allows the musician to perform so perfectly. For an experienced musician, we read in Butler's *Life and Habit*, playing a piece of music has become like breathing: they know it too well to be aware of knowing it, and their conscious attention could not be artificially awakened without compromising the entire performance. In other words, we are only aware of those faculties and skills that we do not yet fully master: conscious attention is but an intermediate stage between perfect mastery and perfect ignorance.[3] The same is true of the ability to write, which we often exercise while we are in the process of thinking about something else: we do so when we take notes and, while jotting down what has just been said, we continue to follow mentally the ongoing speech. It may seem paradoxical, but all this would not be possible without a certain degree of distraction produced by automatism. If we were to pay attention to the shape of the characters or to the movements made by our hands in tracing them, this perfect coordination between the *moi d'habitude* and the *moi de réfléxion* would be compromised.

Therefore, not only does distraction not prevent us from carrying out a series of complex habitual operations in a timely manner, but it also allows us to avoid making mistakes that are often due to excessive attention. For example, as Leopardi observes in *Zibaldone*, under normal conditions, we are perfectly capable of walking in a straight line within two parallel lines drawn on the floor, and we often do so without thinking. However, the situation changes if, for some reason, we start to pay too much attention to them:

> Now suppose that this same space is a beam, or a plank placed like a bridge above a high precipice, or over a river, without protection or supports on any side. How many would not dare to cross on it, or would cross and lose their balance, or would run a much greater risk of losing it! And yet these same people have the faculty and the daily habit of [...] walking the same way every day without losing their balance, when losing their balance is not dangerous.
>
> (*Zibaldone*, 2296–7)

Conscious attention, in this case brought back to the present by the awareness of danger, can suddenly erase an ability that the body, left to itself, would otherwise master to perfection. As Xavier de Maistre observes, "it is easy, when one is performing a mechanical operation, to have one's mind on something else entirely, but it is extremely difficult to watch oneself acting" (*Voyage*, cap. 8, p. 57; Eng. trans. p. 32). Zeno, the protagonist of Italo Svevo's novel, begins to limp as soon as he starts reflecting on the "infernal machine" admirably involved in an action as natural as walking.[4]

For Leopardi, exactly the same thing happens with intellectual operations that involve a degree of automatism, such as reading or listening:

> If you start reading some book, even a very easy one, or listen to the clearest speech in the world, with excessive attention, and an exaggerated concentration of mind, not only does the easy become difficult for you [...], not only do you strive harder to understand than you would have with less attention, not only do you understand less, but, if your attention and the fear of not understanding or of letting something escape is really extreme, you will understand absolutely nothing, as if you hadn't read, and hadn't listened, and as if your mind were completely intent on another matter. For from too much comes nothing, and too much attention to a thing is the equivalent, in effect, of not paying attention [...]. Nor will you be able to gain your purpose unless you relax, and slow down your mind, placing it in a *natural* state, and soothe and put aside your concern to understand.
>
> (*Zibaldone*, 2274–5)

It seems that, within certain limits, some form of distraction or relaxation of the mind is necessary for the exercise and full possession of specific capacities—be they physical or spiritual—that we have acquired through habit. Indeed, the examples of reading and listening are particularly significant, all the more so because these activities are usually associated with concentration. It is precisely to protect the religious man from the dangers of distraction that the monastic rule recommended reading and meditating on sacred books. However, according to the mechanism highlighted here by Leopardi, who was well aware of the fascination and temptations of a cloistered life,[5] a relaxation of attention while reading or listening is not only forgivable but even indispensable for understanding what one is reading or listening to. As we have just read, "from too much comes nothing": excessive attention produces the same effect as lack of attention. Perhaps, paradoxically, it was an excessive effort of attentiveness, rather than its relaxation, that led the monks into temptation by distracting them from a text that had become incomprehensible.

5. The "System of the Soul and the Beast" or the Dangers of Distraction

Distraction is, therefore, as we have said, a luxury brought about by automatism. A luxury for which, however, we pay dearly every time the present surprises us, for example, by placing an unexpected obstacle in our habitual path. It is then that *le moi de réflexion*, abruptly awakened, has just enough time to come back to its senses before it experiences a spectacular fall. However, as Xavier de Maistre shows, this is not the only risk contained in such a mechanism, which he called *le système de l'âme et de la bête* (the system of the soul and the beast).

"I have noticed, through many and sundry observations, that man is made up of a soul and a beast.—These two beings are absolutely distinct, yet so contained within one another, or rather on top of one another, that the soul must in some way be superior to the beast to be able to make such a distinction" (*Voyage*, ch. 6, Fr. 52; Eng. 27). If the soul has "legislative power," the beast on the other hand has "executive power": it is the latter that, not unlike a faithful butler, takes care of preparing lunch, tidying up a room, buttoning a jacket, or guiding our steps toward a usual destination. The ideal, as de Maistre points out, would be to succeed in making the beast so docile and well trained in the execution of these practical functions that the soul, freed from the need to keep it at bay, can trust it to do everything alone so as to indulge freely in its reveries. The space for reverie, in fact, only opens up when the soul can forget about the beast; when the soul is forced to take an interest in what the beast is doing, reverie is impossible.

However, we should lower our expectations: these two beings and their respective powers come into conflict far more often than we would like. There are situations in which the beast, endowed with desires and passions that are never perfectly tamed by habit, can take advantage of the sublime distractions of the soul to let itself get carried away. As de Maistre points out in terms that echo the recent trauma of the French Revolution, the beast can seize the opportunity to oust the legitimate sovereign and claim the right to enjoy its own pleasures:

> Why should you have the right to enjoy yourself without me, all by yourself, on your frequent voyages?—Have I ever objected to your sojourns in the empyrean or in the Elysian Fields, your conversations with invisible intelligences, your profound speculations [...], your castles in the air, your sublime systems?—So why, when you abandon me so, should I not also have the right to enjoy the benefits and pleasures that nature offers me?
>
> (*Voyage*, ch. 39, Fr. 120–1, Eng. 98)

De Maistre mischievously warns us of the risks we run when the soul leaves the beast alone to indulge in its reverie. This is when the beast could lead us to make embarrassing errors that very much look like what we would call today Freudian slips or parapraxis:

> One day last summer I was on my way to the Court. I had been painting all morning, and my soul, taking pleasure in meditating on painting, left it to the beast to transport me to the royal palace.

"What a sublime art painting is!" my soul was thinking. "Happy are the artists moved by the spectacle of nature who are not obliged to make paintings for a living; who do not paint solely as a pastime, but rather, when struck by the majesty of a beautiful countenance or the wonderful play of the light as it blends into a thousand shades on a human face, strive in their works to approximate nature's sublime effects! And happier still the painters who, summoned to their solitary promenades by their love for the landscape, can express on canvas the sadness inspired in them by a shaded thicket or an empty plain. [...]"

As my soul was reflecting thus, the other continued on his way, and God knows where it was going!—Instead of repairing to the court, as it had been ordered to do, it drifted so far to port that by the time my soul caught up, it was at Mme de Hautcastel's front door, a half-mile from the king's palace.

I shall leave it to the reader to imagine what would have happened had I let my beast enter, alone, the house of so lovely a lady.

(*Voyage*, ch. 7, Fr. 55–6, Eng. 29–31)

According to Freud, such lapses almost always reveal the presence of unconfessed thoughts or desires that social pressure forces us to repress. Indeed, as we read in the *Psychopathology of Everyday Life*:

> If I go walking and take a letter with me to be posted, it is not at all necessary that I, as a normal not nervous individual, should carry it in my hand and continually look for a letter-box. As a matter of fact I am accustomed to put it in my pocket and give my thoughts free rein on my way, feeling confident that the first letter-box will attract my attention and cause me to put my hand in my pocket and draw out the letter.[1]

If we forget this intention, Freud maintains, it is probably because we have an unexpressed or unconfessed reason that keeps us from putting it into practice.

And yet carelessness of this kind does not always have the depth of Freudian slips or parapraxis. In some situations, more simply, the soul gives the beast an order to perform something, but is distracted too soon, before it has completed its instructions. For instance, we get up to open the window, but once we are on our feet, we no longer remember what we were supposed to do, and we remain motionless, stunned in the sketch of a suspended action. At first sight, Bergson observes, the explanation of this phenomenon would seem to be rather trivial. We have associated two ideas (that of a purpose to be accomplished and that of a movement to be performed), but then the first idea has vanished, leaving only the representation of the motion. That this is not the case, however, is shown by the fact that it is often by holding this position for a few moments, in which we confusingly feel the urgency of something to be done, that we remember the forgotten intention, as if this intention had tainted the internal image of the movement. This coloring, Bergson points out, would not be the same if the purpose had been different.[2] Similarly, in other cases, it is by retracing our steps or by sitting down again at the work table or in the armchair that we find our forgotten intention—as if the furniture, the corridor, or the position of our body in a given space retained the memory of the initial intention in spite of ourselves. This shows that our psychic life is not made up of discrete and isolated acts of attention that follow and remain external to one another but of a continuum of intertwined sensations, thoughts, images, and movements.

Of course, there are also situations in which, without us being aware of it, the beast automatically carries on, with an entirely different purpose, gestures, or movements whose original intention we have forgotten, as if they did not have at all that particular coloring mentioned by Bergson. As we go to the kitchen to get something from the cupboard, we let ourselves be diverted by the television; struck by a political debate or a scene from a movie, we are suddenly intent on following the program, forgetting the rest. This is essentially what happens to La Bruyère's Ménalque, who systematically forgets what he was doing and why. It is rare for his intentions to remain the same from one end of a corridor or flight of stairs to the other. Regularly lost in his reverie, Ménalque epitomizes the dispersal of a life that lets itself be sidetracked by everything. He begins to tell a story but forgets to finish it and, convinced that he is alone, starts talking and laughing to himself. He asks for information but has already turned away before he can hear the answer, caught up in some other business that has suddenly crossed his mind.[3] In many ways this is what happens to us every time we go on the internet to check our mail or read a message and find ourselves watching a video of an emergency landing in Japan. On closer inspection, however, Ménalque's problem here is not so much distraction as its opposite. Each new stimulus or sensation absorbs his attention completely, concentrating it in a single point and causing the disappearance of all the collateral and coexisting thoughts, sensations, or images that make up our psychic life at every moment.

In Latin, *distrahere* means both "to separate" and "to pull apart." The term "distraction" can therefore indicate both a movement of *separation* and one of *dispersal* and *division*. Referring to this second meaning, Leopardi notes, for example, that distraction often indicates a "multiplicity of attentions"—the multiplicity of things to which one can pay attention at once (*Zibaldone*, 3950–1). Distraction could then be defined as a cognitive state characterized by the *dispersal of attention* over a plurality of objects. We mistakenly tend to think of this state of dispersal and multiplication of attention as a degradation of psychic energy. It seems to us, to take Pierre Janet's example, that an orchestra conductor, capable of paying simultaneous attention to all the instruments, while keeping an eye on the musical score and on the movements of the actors on the stage, must have a great ability to *concentrate* his or her own attention. On the contrary, a conductor makes use precisely of that divided, multiple, and simultaneous attention that, following Leopardi, could be called distraction. It is precisely this capacity that allows them to focus on several things at once.[4]

This kind of distracted attention is actually part of the daily life of our consciousness. This is what Leibniz pointed out with his theory of "small perceptions." In spite of the apparent psychic monotheism, according to which we think of attention as an undivided unit that can be occupied by only one object at a time, our mind is always populated by a crowd of coexisting sensations and ideas—some clearer, some more confused, some completely obscure—to which we simultaneously pay attention in different forms and degrees, very often without realizing it. It is as if, in Ménalque's case, precisely the opposite happens. Every sensation occupies him in an absolute and totalitarian way, canceling out the rest. Having only one idea at a time in his head, he fully identifies with it, translating it with his whole body. This is why, like the actions performed by subjects in a state of hypnosis, Ménalque's gestures lack depth, remain as if foreign to one another, and are not incorporated in what Bergson would call the preexisting "mass of conscious states."[5]

6. Distraction and Somnambulism

Indeed, based on La Bruyère's portrait, Ménalque's character often looks like a sleepwalker who wanders the streets with his eyes closed. Awakened from time to time by an obstacle or the laughter of onlookers, he soon relapses into another dream. During the eighteenth and nineteenth centuries, psychology would often use the comparison with somnambulism (whether natural or induced, as in the case of hypnotism and suggestion) to describe what happens, albeit in a milder form, in moments of distraction or reverie. What somnambulism and distraction have in common is not only, as we have seen, the ability to perform specific operations automatically that would seem to require the presence of a conscious self. Both somnambulism and moments of reverie are characterized by what Pierre Janet called "anesthesia by distraction" (*anesthésie par distraction*): the senses are as if temporarily anaesthetized, resulting in a "constriction" (*rétrécissement*) of the field of consciousness.[1] Janet's views were quite common among thinkers and writers of the nineteenth century. The analogy between distraction and somnambulism could also be found in Maine de Biran (quoted by Janet himself);[2] similarly in a letter to Vieusseux, Leopardi described his habitual tendency to distraction as a state of sensorial suspension: "even in the midst of a conversation [...] I am more *absent*, to put it the English way, than a blind or a deaf person would be."[3]

According to Maine de Biran, this more or less partial suspension of external sensibility depends not so much on a physical cause as on a relaxation of the will or of the self. Sensibility flows back inwards and the exercise of the senses is entirely guided by the imagination. While during wakefulness the imagination is subordinated to the direct impressions of the external senses, in somnambulism and reverie it is the senses that are subordinated to the spontaneous movements of the imagination: "In the first case, the representative picture is arranged or modeled according to the group of real objects that are present to the senses; in the second case, this imaginative picture is given in advance: it is anterior to the objects which are to be adapted to it."[4] Things are no longer perceived through the senses but through the imagination. The distracted person lost in reverie thus behaves like a sleepwalker who, instead of thinking about what they see, sees what they think. Literally, they bend reality to their imagination and, ignoring for a moment the contours of the shared world, they pay attention to external objects only insofar as they show some convenience or resemblance to the inner images that occupy their minds. Objects must make their way into an imaginative framework that erases them and with which they must resonate in order to be perceived.

That is why when we are distracted and lost in reverie, we may not recognize a person in the street. Abandoned to a purely passive vision, the eyes—to quote a beautiful image by Maine de Biran—merely reflect images outside themselves, like the smooth surface of a mirror.[5] Indeed, the eyes of those lost in thought often take on a glassy, expressionless quality. This is how, for example, Manzoni describes the distracted eyes of Gertrude (whom some view as an Italian version of Madame Bovary), which often were "motionless and inattentive," revealing "the laboring of concealed thought, the effort to overcome some secret feeling of her soul, which had more power over it than all surrounding objects."[6] This is also how Manet depicts the fixed, absent gaze of the barmaid at the counter of the *Folies Bergère* in Paris (Figure 2): her distracted, detached expression separates her

Figure 2 Édouard Manet, *Un bar aux Folies Bergère*, 1882, London, The Courtauld Gallery. Copyright © 2022 by Art UK.

from the whirlwind of life in the bar reflected in the mirror behind her—a mirror in which the painter perhaps also lets us guess, through a false perspective, the reverie in which she is engaged. And when they are not motionless, the eyes of the distracted person wander carelessly over the surrounding objects, like sunlight on a wall. Such were the gazes that, in Balbec, Albertine and her friends carelessly placed on the narrator of *À la recherche du temps perdu* before making his acquaintance: "these eyes, whose incomprehensible gaze struck me from time to time and played unwittingly upon me like an effect of sunlight upon a wall."[7]

Something similar happens with hearing. A distracted person ceases for a moment to listen to the voices and sounds around them. Words themselves stop having a meaning and become part of an indistinct background hum. Thus, the person who is lost in their thoughts does not (or not immediately) hear a voice calling their name. The proverbial distraction of scientists, perfectly embodied by Archimedes (almost the Ménalque of scientists, considering the many episodes of absent-mindedness he inspired), seems to consist in this temporary constriction of the field of consciousness. It is said that when he was absorbed in solving a geometry problem, Archimedes failed to notice the siege of Syracuse, during which he was barbarously killed.[8] Maybe as a warning against the dangers of distraction produced by over-intensive study, between the seventeenth and nineteenth centuries this scene, in which a Roman soldier comes up behind the unsuspecting mathematician, was emblematically reproduced by many artists, including Delacroix, whose painting decorates the ceiling of the Bibliothèque du Palais Bourbon in Paris (see Figure 3).

It seems, however, that even in such cases the mind still retains a minimal degree of attention. Sometimes, when coming back to ourselves, we are able to remember what the other person has just said, the imprint of which is nonetheless present in our consciousness – a sign, therefore, that we had heard their words, albeit without

Figure 3 Eugène Delacroix, *Archimède tué par le soldat*, 1839–47, ceiling, Bibliothèque du Palais Bourbon, Paris. Copyright © 2022 by Assemblée Nationale.

consciously paying attention to them. Bergson gives a particularly appropriate example of this:

> Whilst I am writing these lines, the hour strikes on a neighboring clock, but my inattentive ear does not perceive it until several strokes have made themselves heard. Hence I have not counted

them; and yet I only have to turn my attention backwards to count up the four strokes which have already sounded and add them to those which I hear. If, then, I question myself carefully on what has just taken place, I perceive that the first four sounds had struck my ear and even affected my consciousness, but that the sensations produced by each one of them, instead of being set side by side, had melted into one another in such a way as to give the whole a peculiar quality, to make a kind of musical phrase out of it.[9]

Without becoming fully conscious, bells still strike the attention of those absorbed in other thoughts. Although they are not perceived in their discrete and quantitative aspect (which would require the exercise of voluntary and conscious attention), they are nevertheless registered as an intensive multiplicity in terms of duration. It is for this reason that, as Proust notes, childhood reading "leaves behind in us above all the image of the places and days where and when we engaged in it,"[10] the memory of which somehow remained attached like an aura to the pages we read.

This shows once again that attention is a much more complex and polymorphous phenomenon than it is usually thought to be. It is not something absolute, whole, and indivisible, which is either given or not—like a light switch that is either on or off. Attention is a plural, extensive phenomenon, composed of degrees and nuances, and not at all incompatible with distraction. Rather than a beam of light that we shine on specific objects, leaving everything else in complete shadow, attention might instead be compared to a photographic plate that can be affected in various ways.[11]

7. Reverie and the History of Madness

During the eighteenth century, many physicians influenced by Locke's philosophy sought the origin of madness in an alteration of sensibility.[1] If the insane see or hear things that are different from those that are part of the common experience of other people (if, for example, as we read in Diderot and d'Alembert's *Encyclopédie*, they hear choirs of angels, in the manner of some enthusiasts, or mistake windmills for giants, as in the case of Don Quixote), this depends primarily on an alteration of "the right relationship between our sensations and physical objects."[2] To quote the image with which Voltaire summarizes these views, madness depends not so much on a defect in the soul as on the fact that "the windows of its dwelling are sealed" or in a bad state. This is why the insane have lost "common sense."[3] Madness, in other words, would be nothing more than a form of hallucination: a peripheral and non-centralized disorder, which as such does not affect the intellect and the ability to think.

Indeed, as Locke observed: "For [the insane] do not appear to me to have lost the faculty of reasoning: but having joined together some ideas very wrongly, they mistake them for truths; and they err as men do, that argue right from wrong principles." This is proven by the fact that, after "having taken their fancies for realities, they make right deductions from them." So we could find "a *distracted man* fancying himself a king, with a right inference, require suitable attendance, respect, and obedience. Others who have thought themselves made of glass, have used the caution necessary to preserve such brittle bodies" (*Essay*, II, ch. 11, § 13, my emphasis). In the first of his *Metaphysical Meditations*, Descartes used these same examples to emphasize the absolute extravagance of the insane, who come to conceive the most absurd things; Locke, on the contrary, uses them to show the full reasonableness of their conduct. Their behavior appears bizarre and extravagant only to those who observe it from the outside, but if we were to pay attention to what goes on in their head (to what they are thinking or believe they are seeing at that moment), their behavior would be entirely reasonable.[4]

According to this view, the insane are literally, to quote Locke, "distracted" people, that is, people disconnected from reality and the shared world.⁵ Their madness is a form of hallucination caused by the poor state of the "windows" through which light enters the dark room of their minds.⁶ The mind of the insane, like that of a sleeper, is as if withdrawn from the senses and can be described with the words of Heraclitus: "The world of the waking is one and shared, but the sleeping turn aside each into their own private world."⁷ From this point of view, both dream and reverie are to all intents and purposes a true form of madness that we all experience every day, albeit mildly and temporarily.⁸

While the analogy between dreams and madness has often been stressed, the almost forgotten affinity between madness and reverie proves more interesting. In fact, it can help us to understand better the place of distraction and reverie in our culture. It is worth asking whether they are not, in fact, a form of madness—"libertinism of the mind" (*libertinage d'esprit*), as Diderot put it⁹—that Western reason inadvertently tolerated within itself when it chose to banish madness as something other and absolutely negative. In this view, reverie can be seen as one of the many fragments into which what Foucault called madness in its "wild state"¹⁰ (the constellation of experiences that constituted it before its systematization) has been dispersed and dissolved.

As La Bruyère pointed out with his portrait of Ménalque, in the seventeenth century it was not always easy to distinguish the distracted individual from other social figures. Ménalque, as we read in *Les Caractères* (*Characters*), could easily appear stupid because he does not listen to or interact with others, or inconsiderate because he discusses bankruptcy and other disasters in the presence of people who have been affected by them. He could also be mistaken for an ill-mannered person because he walks by without saying hello, and finally for a madman, because he talks to himself and his face often contracts into grimaces or unjustified expressions.¹¹ This is why La Bruyère's text is constructed through a fast-paced series of scenes and episodes—more like sketches or vignettes—that follow one another without a narrative center or development, as if to *test* (rather than define) distraction in all possible situations and contexts. This procedure, which Bergson judged excessive, is in fact an integral part of La Bruyère's cognitive method, as Barthes pointed out.[12] In the single isolated episode, the identity of the distracted person seems to crystallize for a moment and coincide with other possible social figures. Hence the importance of enumeration and seriality, which highlight points of tangency and overlap, while avoiding misunderstandings and taking Ménalque for what he is not.

It is in particular the overlap with the madman that interests us here, as evidence of the fact that the boundaries between these two figures were still fluid and undecided at the time.[13] There is, in other words, an obvious family resemblance between Ménalque and Don Quixote, between reverie and madness. Still detectable in the seventeenth and eighteenth centuries, this similarity would gradually tend to disappear. However, it can help us to clarify the role of distraction in our culture or, more precisely, the reasons and social mechanisms for its condemnation and rejection.

8. Madness, Distraction, and Common Sense: On the Political and Aesthetic Dimension of Distraction and Reverie

In the *Encyclopédie*, "madness" (*folie*) is defined as a departure from reason, which consists in nothing other than the knowledge of truth. This truth, however, should not be confused with "that truth which the author of nature has reserved for himself alone, which he has placed beyond the reach of our mind." The truth from which the insane are excluded is, instead, "that sensible truth, that truth which is within the reach of all human beings and which they have the ability to know, because it is necessary to them, either for the preservation of their being, or for their particular happiness, or for the general good of society."[1] According to this criterion, a madman is someone who does not participate in the "sensible truth" and does not see what everyone else sees, as happens to Don Quixote when he mistakes a herd of sheep for the army of the emperor Alifanfaron. Rather than conformity between sensations and external objects, the "sensible truth" from which the insane deviate is defined as conformity between our sensations and those of others, or rather those of the majority.

That is why, the entry in the *Encyclopédie* goes on to say, perhaps the mad people who are locked up "only differ from the rest of humanity because their follies are of a less common kind, and do not fall within the order of society." The latter consists of nothing other than the "combination of human follies" and socially accepted follies are of two types.[2] On the one hand, the kind that is considered useful for individual and collective well-being. On the other hand, the kind that, while having no particular use, is common to a large number of individuals and, for obvious reasons, cannot be banished from human society. The truth from which madness would depart is thus defined on the basis of a purely statistical and quantitative criterion. What identifies madness is, more than its opposition to the truth, its supposedly antisocial character; the insane person is someone who is affected by a less common form of madness. The "sensible truth" on which society is built is nothing more than the set of socially useful and shared forms of madness, which are "true" only in this sense.

Like a madman, a distracted person lost in thought does not partake in the experience shared by other people—of that "sensible truth" which, as we have seen, consists in the perfect conformity between our perceptions and those of the majority. The problem of the distracted person is not so much a lack of attention as the fact that they do not see what everyone else sees because they are paying attention to something else. The "sensible truth" that the distracted person disregards could then be defined as a specific distribution of the visible and the sensible determined by what society pays attention to. The distracted person does not participate in the dominant distribution of the sensible because they are disconnected from the general concertation and synchronization of collective attention. Their distraction is precisely what prevents them from thinking and acting in unison with other people.

As Bergson observed, living in society requires that we pay attention to what society itself requires us to pay attention to. In particular, road signs, shop closing times or school opening times, the latest news, weather forecasts, public holidays, daylight saving time, the presence of unattended luggage or dodgy faces (the ever present announcement in British train stations, "if you see something that doesn't look right […], see it, say it, sorted"),[3] the ringing of a telephone, stock market trends, advertisements for the best deals, and, in general, useful and productive activities as opposed to idle and unproductive ones. In this sense, as well as being a "combination of human follies," society can also be defined as an arrangement of collective attention, which guarantees the existence of a common and shared perceptual world, made up of a precise division of space, a distribution of roles and objects, and a subdivision of the activities to which it is legitimate or illegitimate to pay attention. In this sense, distraction coincides, as Bergson stresses, with a form of *unsociability* that society punishes and suppresses.[4] But in so doing, society also punishes and represses the potentially subversive and dissensual scope of this mental attitude, which is sometimes capable of making visible what society itself does not want us to see or pay attention to.

By carrying out an "inversion of common sense,"[5] a distracted gaze can reconfigure the "sensible truth" imposed by dominant attention—that "everyone knows" (*tout le monde sait*) which, according to Deleuze, is the implicit assumption of "common sense," often embraced and validated also by philosophy. For Deleuze, this assumption is "dogmatic" because it is taken for granted, viewed as "natural," and presupposed as the result of a natural exercise of thought spontaneously in tune with truth. This assumption is also "moral" because it always promotes specific forms of representation and recognition which convey received values and hierarchies.[6]

The gaze of a distracted person can reveal how the acts of looking, seeing, or listening (generally considered passive operations) are in fact *active*, not only cognitively, but also aesthetically and politically. They are cognitively active operations because, as observed for instance by Maine de Biran (almost anticipating Taine's hypothesis on the hallucinatory nature of all external perception, defined as "true hallucination"), very often we perceive through our imagination and not through our senses. This mechanism, which allows us to explain, for example, why we see ghosts, comes into play not only in the phenomena of instinct and habit but also when we see from a distance a blurred and shapeless object, whose contours the eye cannot make out. If someone tells us that what we are seeing is such and such an object (say, an animal), *then* we begin to recognize its shape, size, dimension, etc. In other words, external perception is never a simple act that derives solely from the relationship with external objects.[7] Furthermore, our sensory perception is also aesthetically and politically active: as noted in particular by Jacques Rancière, every way of looking always brings about the capacity to *confirm* or *transform* a specific division and distribution of the sensible (what he calls *le partage du sensible*). And, as stressed by Yves Citton, it is first of all what we pay attention to that shapes how we look.[8]

La Bruyère, as we have seen, was perhaps one of the first to explore the aesthetic and political dimension of distraction in the section of *Les Caractères* dedicated to Ménalque. In the various situations in which it is presented (scenes which could fit for Laurel and Hardy or a Jacques Tati film), distraction systematically, albeit always accidentally, unfolds its subversive power, creating a democratic space where the most diverse objects and characters find themselves on the same level and end up swapping roles.⁹ By suspending the usual coordinates of meaning, which Ménalque forgets, ignores, or misunderstands, distraction cancels the implicit hierarchies and separations that regulate and justify particular behaviors and social conventions. Similarly, Ménalque's trespassing on the borders between different social places—such as church and bedroom, court and city—disrupts the traditional division of spaces and objects, emphasizing the equivalence and continuity between places traditionally kept separate and thought of as heterogeneous.¹⁰

During a lecture given at the University of Oxford in 1911, entitled *La perception du changement* (The Perception of Change), Bergson observed that the purpose of art (and, following art, also of philosophy) is precisely to produce distraction. Bergson gives the example of Corot and Turner: it is mistakenly thought that these painters present us with the products of their imagination, through which we would be transported to another reality. It is not at all in this sense that art produces distraction. What Corot and Turner achieve with their paintings is a radical *conversion* of attention which, by diverting it from its practical function and turning it toward that which is useless (*ce qui ne sert à rien*), suddenly shows the spectators what they normally perceive without being aware of it. Thus, a Turner painting allows us to grasp the continuous change behind the seeming immobility of forms and colors.

Whether it is painting, sculpture, poetry, or music, art for Bergson has no other purpose than to "show us, in nature and in the mind, outside of us and within us, things which did not explicitly strike our senses and our consciousness,"¹¹ freeing us, if only temporarily, from the commonsensical generalizations, representational conventions, and prejudices that preemptively steer our attention (Benjamin would say something similar about photography and cinema¹²). The fact is that the artist, for Bergson, is a distracted person, someone whose senses (if not all of them, at least one, which determines their predisposition toward a given art form) have been accidentally, and as if by mistake, disconnected or detached by nature from their practical function: "Not with that intentional, logical, systematical detachment—the result of reflection and philosophy—but rather with a natural detachment, one innate in the structure of sense or consciousness, which at once reveals itself by a virginal manner, so to speak, of seeing, hearing, or thinking."[13]

Deleuze will say something similar in relation to philosophy, which is not born from an act of goodwill but from the intrusion of something fortuitous that forces us to think, from the contingency of an encounter that confronts us with a new problem. Common sense, where everything is given in advance and arranged to be recognized, is precisely what makes encounters impossible. Encounters are made by chance, out of distraction. And when they occur, more than awareness, what they provoke is the affirmation of a new sensibility, of a different way of looking and seeing that overturns common sense and introduces a different distribution of the sensible and the intelligible. This is why, as Deleuze reiterates, "there is only involuntary thought"[14] and philosophers, or rather the best philosophers, are idle, or (we might add) distracted.

9. Distraction and Idleness

Like madness, distraction always acquires its meaning within a given culture or society that recognizes and identifies it as such, insofar as it implies psychological and moral modes of conduct that do not fit in with those shared by the majority. In the specific case of distraction, this occurs starting from the modalities of attention that a specific culture or society demands from its members. The various religious, philosophical, medical, psychological, or sociological analyses that for centuries have continued to banish distraction, either by treating it as a sin or by diagnosing it as a disease or a disorder of attention, are above all projections of cultural themes that indirectly reveal the customs, values, and implicit assumptions of a given society.[1]

Of course, there are situations where it is essential to be attentive to what everyone else is paying attention to (if you are driving a car, you should pay attention to traffic signs, unless perhaps you have a self-driving vehicle). However, very often distraction simply means paying attention to the wrong thing—to something other than what the authorities want us to pay attention to.[2] Think of a distracted schoolchild in the classroom, of Madame Bovary daydreaming during mass, of Julien Sorel reading a book astride a wooden beam instead of working in his father's sawmill, or of Baudelaire's poet contemplating the clouds while letting his soup go cold.[3] These examples suggest how the social condemnation of distraction is often motivated by an unexpressed yet evident reason, which once again leads us to consider the affinity between reverie and madness.

As Foucault showed, the history of madness was, for an important stretch of its tortuous course, an integral part of the proscription of idleness and laziness. A vice par excellence within the emerging bourgeois universe, in the seventeenth-century idleness became—in its unproductive nature—the "worst of all possible revolts," which motivated the internment of all those who, for various reasons, were incapable of taking part in the production of common wealth: the insane, the poor, invalids, beggars, the unemployed, libertines, those with venereal diseases, etc. Rather than treatment, the purpose of imprisonment, which often included forced labor, was primarily the removal of social groups perceived as parasitic and unproductive.[4] The moral and social condemnation that still hovers around distraction today is not so different from that which, in the seventeenth century, began to surround madness. The condemnation of distraction has also been—and in many ways still is—an integral part of this centuries-old proscription of idleness and laziness. No less than the insane, the distracted are also considered fundamentally incompatible with a social order dominated by the imperative of work and maximum productivity. After all, those who are truly distracted also pay little attention to entertainments or amusements, that is, to those forms of socially controlled and permitted distraction that are nothing but ways of preemptively structuring and exploiting our free attention.[5]

Conclusion: Distraction and Laughter

At the end of the last part of this book we saw how the social condemnation of distraction is in many ways akin—albeit in a milder form—to the condemnation and banishment of madness in our culture. Laughter is one of the most obvious social mechanisms of reproach and exclusion of distraction. Why do we laugh at someone who is distracted? What is so funny about distraction? There are many possible explanations, but the disciplining role that laughter often plays in relation to distraction certainly cannot be ignored.

As Bergson pointed out, laughter is a social gesture that responds to particular requirements of communal life. It has both a normative and a corrective function: "What life and society require of each of us is a constantly alert attention that discerns the outlines of the present situation, together with a certain elasticity of mind and body to enable us to adapt ourselves in consequence."[1] Laughter serves precisely to restrain the "eccentricity" of particular ways of behaving, repressing any "separatist tendency" that conflicts with the order of society. From this point of view, distraction represents, according to Bergson, a "slight form of revolt" that laughter is meant to suppress.[2] More precisely, laughter is the means by which society punishes distracted people for paying attention to something other than what they are supposed to. Thus we laugh at the philosopher who falls into a well while looking at the stars,[3] just as we laugh at Don Quixote who, having read too many chivalric romances, ends up losing sight of reality.

According to Bergson, it would be a mistake to think that the comedy of these cloud-headed individuals lies simply in the meaninglessness of their actions. The target of our laughter is rather the detachment of their actions from the social context, more precisely from the goals and priorities prescribed by society. We would not laugh if the same philosopher fell into the well in order to perform some heroic action. What we mercilessly laugh at is the fact that the philosopher falls into the well to look at the stars—the quintessential example of a dreamer's idle activity. It is significant, from this point of view, that we laugh at people but not at animals (except when the latter are humanized and express attitudes that recall human ones). Bergson would agree with Leopardi that the most accurate philosophical definition of the human is not as a "rational animal" but rather as an *animale risibile*—not so much, however, in the sense of "animal which laughs" as of "animal which provokes laughter."[4]

In analyzing the social mechanisms of laughter, Bergson focuses primarily on the matter of automatism. The mechanical obstinacy of a distracted person, who impassibly continues doing what they were doing even if circumstances dictate otherwise, triggers laughter since in this case distraction reveals a form of hardening or rigidity with respect to a social life that wants us not only to be focused but also to be flexible and adaptable. However, if we look more closely, the eccentricity that society seeks to correct and banish through laughter concerns not so much automatism but rather the state of reverie that it indirectly reveals—the fact that the distracted person has taken the liberty of thinking about something else. Society always wants us to be attentive and attuned to the present, but automatism, as we saw in the last chapter, is often the external facet of reverie and therefore of a mental space that escapes social control.

As Bergson recognizes, the distracted actions of cloud-headed people are never simple "cases of *absence of mind*, pure and simple."[5]

As we have seen, reverie is a luxury we allow ourselves when we have achieved perfect automatism in performing a given activity; automatism dispenses us from the need to keep an eye on the present and on what we are doing and frees up mental space for us to direct our attention elsewhere. By inviting us to "multitask," society would like to take possession of this opaque and unproductive mental space and put it to work. The laughter that breaks out when, lost in reverie, we rely on automatism and end up stumbling over an unexpected obstacle, serves to remind us that even that mental space belongs to society by rights. A similar point could be made about the comedy of some slips of the tongue, where we distractedly reveal what we are really thinking. Perhaps what arouses laughter is precisely the fact that we betray ourselves at the very moment we wanted to betray society, unintentionally revealing thoughts that we would have preferred to keep hidden from it, escaping its desire for total transparency. As in Chris Marker's film *La Jetée*, the ideal police would be one that could spy even on people's dreams.

However, there is, fortunately, also another sense in which laughter may have to do with distraction. As Bergson suggests toward the end of his essay, sometimes, even if only for a moment, we happen to identify with the distracted person. We sometimes feel close to them and put ourselves in their place. Laughter can then arise from this identification as a *détente* (relaxation). Remaining always attentive to and connected with the social world requires constant effort, a permanent intellectual tension from which it is pleasurable to be relieved from time to time. Laughter thus offers the possibility of escaping, together with the distracted person, from this effort and this continuous tension. The attention we owe to life and society is loosened, and for a moment we participate in the dreaming, the playfulness, and the laziness of those who are distracted. In this case, laughter is no longer a means of punishment or correction, but the suspension of any immediate and interested relationship with our surroundings; it is a relaxation and distraction of the mind.[6] Then we no longer laugh at the distracted person but rather at the senselessness of the codes they have unwittingly broken.

Notes

Introduction 1

1. Originally from Luxemburg, Hugo Gernsback (1884–1967) moved to the United States in 1904 and is primarily recognized today for his contribution to the formation and definition of the science-fiction genre, along with Edgar Allan Poe, Jules Verne, and H. G. Wells, of whom he was an admirer. He was also a technician, scientist, and inventor specialized in electrical equipment. His most notable inventions include the first home radio set and the first walkie-talkie. On Hugo Gernsback and his work, see Grant Wythoff, *The Perversity of Things: Hugo Gernsback on Media, Tinkering, and Scientifiction* (Minneapolis, MN: University of Minnesota Press, 2016), which also includes a collection of some of Gernsback's most representative writings, Gary Westfahl, *The Mechanics of Wonder. The Creation of the Idea of Science Fiction* (Liverpool: Liverpool University Press, 1998), and Garyn G. Roberts, "Hugo Gernsback," in *American Magazine Journalists, 1900–1960*, ed. Sam G. Riley (Detroit, MI: Gale Research, 1994), 96–103.
2. Hugo Gernsback, "The Isolator," *Science and Invention* 13, n. 3 (July 1925), quoted from Wythoff, *The Perversity of Things*, 284–6.
3. Ibid.
4. A recreation of this room is found at the Musée Carnavalet in Paris.
5. See for instance Dominic Pettnam, *Infinite Distraction. Paying Attention to Social Media* (Cambridge: Polity Press, 2016). For a criticism of the idea of "weapons of mass distraction," see *infra*, my Introduction to the Italian edition.
6. For a critical discussion of this perspective, see Enrico Campo, *Attention and Its Crisis in Digital Society*, trans. Ian Richard (New York: Routledge, 2022).

7 For a similar perspective, see also Marina van Zuylen, *The Plenitude of Distraction* (New York: Sequence Press, 2017).

8 See David Marno, *Death Be Not Proud: The Art of Holy Attention* (Chicago and London: The University of Chicago Press, 2017), Introduction and ch. 4.

9 For an enquiry concerning the temporal disorders arising from modernity, see in particular Elissa Marder, *Dead Time: Temporal Disorders in the Wake of Modernity (Baudelaire and Flaubert)* (Stanford: Stanford University Press, 2001).

10 Maybe the problem with Pascal's view is of having introduced a seemingly inescapable alternative between distraction and ennui, which are mistakenly thought of as opposites.

11 See Jonathan Crary, *24/7. Late Capitalism and the End of Sleep* (New York: Verso, 2013), the culmination of a thirty-year-long research project on the problem of perception and attention, which includes *Techniques of the Observer. On Vision and Modernity in the Nineteenth Century* (Cambridge, MA: MIT Press, 1990), and *Suspensions of Perception: Attention, Perception, and Modern Culture* (Cambridge, MA: MIT Press, 2001).

12 In this sense, we could say of distraction, what Bergson said about "disorder." If we enter a room that has not been tidied up (*rangée*), we say that it is in a state of "disorder" because we do not notice the "order of life" that manifests itself in the room (the remains of a meal, some books left open on the table, a half-emptied glass, a jacket on the chair) (see Henri Bergson, *L'Évolution créatrice* [Paris: Presses Universitaires de France, 1948], ch. 3, trans. Arthur Mitchell, *Creative Evolution* [London: Electric Book, 2001]). In other words, as Bergson points out, we call "disorder" (lack of order) the manifestation of an order we are not interested in. Likewise, we often call distraction (lack of attention) a type of attention that simply does not interest us because it has no recognizable use.

13 For the religious origins of this idea of attention that, in any given instant, can only focus on one thing, see Marno, *Death Be Not Proud*, according to which this ideal was formed in the early centuries of

Christianity and is later found in early modern philosophy, namely in Descartes and Malebranche. It is in Augustine in particular that attention becomes "this moving and selective stretching towards that which it has selected" (ibid., 142).

14 As Agamben observes, "Deleuze once defined the operation of power [*potere*, in the sense of "authority" or "dominance"] as a separation of humans from what they can do, from their potentiality [*potenza*] [...]. There is, nevertheless, another and more insidious operation of power that does not immediately affect what humans can do—their potentiality—but rather their 'impotentiality', that is what they cannot do, or better, can not do [*ciò che non possono fare o, meglio, possono non fare*]. That potentiality is always also constitutively an impotentiality, that every ability to do is also always an ability to not do, is the decisive point of the theory of potentiality developed by Aristotle in the ninth book of *Metaphysics*. 'Impotentiality [*adynamia*],' he writes, 'is a privation contrary to potentiality [*dynamis*]. Every potentiality is impotentiality of the same [potentiality]' (1046a30-31). 'Impotentiality' does not mean here only absence of potentiality, not being able to do, but also and above all 'being able to not do,' being able to not exercise one's own potentiality. And indeed, it is precisely this specific ambivalence of all potentialities—which is always the power to be and to not be, to do and to not do—that defines, in fact, human potentiality [...]. This [...] permits human beings to accumulate and freely master their own capacity, to transform them into 'faculties'. It is not only the measure of what someone can do, but also and primarily the capacity of maintaining oneself in relation to own's own possibility to not do, that defines the status of one's action" (Giorgio Agamben, "Su ciò che possiamo non fare," in *Nudità* [Roma: Nottetempo, 2009], 67–8, trans. David Kishik and Stefan Pedatella, "On What We Can Not Do," in *Nudities* [Stanford: Stanford University Press, 2011], 43–4).

15 Paul North, *The Problem of Distraction* (Stanford: Stanford University Press, 2012) tries to escape the "tautological nature" of the concept of distraction (always implicitly bound and subordinated to attention) by introducing the idea of a "non-attentional distraction," defined as

"not-always thinking" or "periodic non-thought" (ibid., 6–7). He finds it in Aristotle's "image of an intermitted interruption of cognition," in La Bruyère's figure of Ménalque, later identified with "le distrait" (the distracted person), as well as in Franz Kafka, Martin Heidegger, and Walter Benjamin. While my perspective draws on North's for many important insights, however, I see distraction as a positive capacity and not the negation of thought. For an analysis of the problems of attention and distraction in German culture, see also the volume recently published by Carolin Duttlinger, *Attention and Distraction in Modern German Literature, Thought, and Culture* (Oxford: Oxford University Press, 2022).

16 See Simone Weil, *La consition ouvrière* (Paris: Gallimard, 1951), 202–3.
17 Likewise, in the film *Modern Times* by Charlie Chaplin (particularly appreciated by Simone Weil) the worker on the assembly line does not even have the time to shoo away a fly that is buzzing next to him, disturbing his work: in other words, he has no time for distraction.
18 See also Elena Sofia Arpe, "Il compito politico della distrazione," *Intersezioni* XLII, n. 2 (August 2022): 213–27, which analyzes the political and aesthetical dimension of distraction with special reference to Martin Heidegger, Oskar Becker, and Giorgio Agamben. According to Arpe, distraction allows what Agamben has called "profanation."
19 See J.-M. Le Clézio, *L'Extase matérielle* (Paris: Gallimard, 1967).
20 See Massimo Carboni, *La mosca di Dreyer. L'opera della contingenza nelle arti* (Milan: Jaka Books, 2007).

Introduction 2

1 "Though they do talk with you, and seem to be otherwise employed, and to your thinking very intent and busy, still that toy runs in their mind, that fear, that suspicion, that abuse, that jealousy, that agony, that vexation, that cross, that castle in the air, that crotchet, that whimsy, that fiction, that pleasant waking dream, whatsoever it is […]. They do not much heed what you say, their mind is on another matter; ask what you will, they do not attend, or much intend that business they

are about, but forget themselves what they are saying, doing, or should otherwise say or do, whither they are going, distracted with their own melancholy thoughts" (Robert Burton, *The Anatomy of Melancholy*, eds. Thomas C. Faulkner, Nicolas K. Kiessling, and Rhonda L. Blair [Oxford: Oxford University Press, 1989, vol. 1], 393).

2   See Pettman, *Infinite Distraction*.
3   See Théodule Ribot, *Psychologie de l'attention* (Pais: Félix Alcan, Paris, 1889), 115, trans. *The Psychology of Attention*, authorized translation (London: Longmans, Green, & Co., 1890).
4   See Henri Bergson, *Essai sur les données immédiates de la conscience*, ed. Frédéric Worms (Paris: Presses Universitaires de Frances, 2013), ch. 1, 11–3, trans. Frank Lubecki Pogson, *Time and Free Will: An Essay on the Immediate Data of Consciousness* (New York: Dover Publication, 2012).
5   Stendhal, *De l'amour*, ed. Victor Del Litto (Paris: Gallimard, 1980), ch. XIV, 54–5, and ch. XVI, 57, trans. Gilbert and Suzanne Sale, *Love* (London: Penguin, 2004).
6   See Marcel Proust, "Sur la lecture," in *Écrits sur l'art*, ed. Jérôme Picon (Paris: Flammarion, 1999), 187–224, trans. Damion Searls, *On Reading* (London: Hesperus Press Limited, 2011). This text, which is part of the preface that Proust wrote for his translation of John Ruskin's *Sesame and Lilies*, initially appeared in *La Renaissance latine* on 15 June 1905 and was then taken up again under the title of "Journées de lecture."
7   It probably is in this sense that we should understand Roland Barthes's remark in *Le plaisir du texte* (Paris: Seuil, 1973), 41–2, trans. Richard Miller, *The Pleasure of the Text* (New York: Hill and Wang, 1975), 24–5: "To be with the one I love and to think of something else: this is how I have my best ideas, how I best invent what is necessary to my work. Likewise for the text: it produces, in me, the best pleasure if it manages to make itself heard indirectly; if, reading it, I am led to look up often, to listen to something else. I am not necessarily *captivated* by the text of pleasure; it can be an act that is slight, complex, tenuous, almost scatterbrained: a sudden movement of the head, like a bird who understands nothing of what we hear, who hears what we do not understand." See also Michael Wood, *Habits of Distraction* (Brighton: Sussex Academic, 2011), 21–33.

8   Gilles Deleuze, *Pourparlers. 1972-1990* (Paris: Les Éditions de Minuit, 1990/2003), 236, trans. Martin Joughin, *Negotiations. 1972-1990* (New York: Columbia University Press, 1995), 174.

9   Ibid., Fr. 238, Eng. 175. See also ibid., Fr. 176-7, Eng. 129, where Deleuze writes: "We sometimes go on as though people can't express themselves. In fact, they are always expressing themselves [...]. So it is not a problem of getting people to express themselves but to provide little gaps of solitude and silence in which they might eventually find something to say. Repressive forces don't stop people expressing themselves but rather force them to express themselves. What a relief to have nothing to say, the right to say nothing, because only then there is a chance of framing the rare, and ever rarer, thing that might be worth saying." On "control societies" see also Bernard E. Harcourt, *Exposed. Desire and Disobedience in the Digital Age* (Cambridge, MA: Harvard University Press, 2015), according to which our "control societies" also work as "expository societies" (as societies of exposure and exhibition), based not so much on obligation and coercion as on the exploitation of our desires and passions.

10 See Yves Citton, "Économie de l'attention et nouvelles exploitations numériques," *Multitudes* 3, n. 54 (2013): 163-75, and *Pour une écologie de l'attention* (Paris: Seuil, 2014), trans. Barnaby Norman, *The Ecology of Attention* (Cambridge: Polity Press, 2016). See also *L'économie de l'attention*, ed. Yves Citton (Paris: La Découverte, 2014).

11 See Citton, "Attention collective et vigilance médiatique," in *Intellecta. Revue de l'Association pour la Recherche Cognitive*, n. 66 (2016/2): 161-80 and Gilles Deleuze, *Le bergsonisme* (Paris: Presses Universitaires de Frances, 1966), 111-9, trans. Hugh Tomlinson and Barbara Habberjam, *Bergsonism* (New York: Zone Books, 1990).

Part 1

1   See Pascal, *Pensées*, ed. P. Sellier (Paris: Bordas, coll. "Classiques Garnier", 1991), fr. 33 and 198, trans. Honor Levi, Pascal, *Pensées and Other Writings*, ed. Anthony Levi (Oxford and New York: Oxford

University Press, 1995). Henceforth *Pensées* followed by the number of the fragment.

2   See Heidegger, *Sein und Zeit* (Halle: Max Niemeyer, 1927), trans. John Macquarrie and Edward Robinson, *Being and Time* (New York: Harper & Row, 1962). For a comparison between Pascal's anthropology and the existential analytic of *Being and Time*, see in particular Jean Brun, *La philosophie de Pascal* (Paris: Presses Universitaires de France, 1992), 67 et seq., and Vincent Carraud, *Pascal et la philosophie* (Paris: Presses Universitaires de France, 1992), 453.

3   See Giorgio Agamben, *Stanze. La parola e il fantasma nella cultura occidentale* (Turin: Einaudi, 1977), trans. Ronald L. Martinez, *Stanzas: Word and Phantasm in Western Culture* (Minneapolis; London: University of Minnesota Press, 1993).

4   See "Ennui," in *Encyclopédie ou dictionnaire raisonné des sciences, des arts et des métiers*, eds. Denis Diderot and Jean Le Rond d'Alembert, 28 vols. (Paris: Le Breton, Michel-Antoine David, Laurent Durand, & Antoine-Claude Briasson, 1751–1772), vol. 6 (1756). On the evolution of the meaning of the French word *ennui* from the seventeenth to the nineteenth centuries, and on its adoption into English, see Richard Scholar, *Émigrés: French Words That Turned English* (Princeton, NJ: Princeton University Press, 2020), 130–64.

5   Pierre Nicole's letter, probably written soon after the publication of Pascal's *Pensées*, bears the following title: "On the praise which a person of spirit has given of Mr. Pascal's *Pensées*, without making known, and perhaps without knowing herself, their actual merits" (see Pierre Nicole, *Continuation Des Essais De Morale* (Paris: Guillaume Desprez, 1755), vol. VIII, Lettre LXXXVIII, 243–7). The person in question is indeed Madame de Lafayette. Nicole probably wrote this letter in response to a comment made by Madame de Lafayette on Pascal's *Pensées* in a letter now lost. For a discussion of this letter, see Edward D. James, *Pierre Nicole, Jansenist and Humanist: A Study of His Thought* (The Hague: Martinus Nijhoff, 1972), 110–2.

6   See Martin Heidegger, *Die Grundbegriffe der Metaphysik: Welt – Endlichkeit – Einsamkeit* (Frankfurt am Main: V. Klostermann, 1983), trans. William McNeill and Nicholas Walker, *The Fundamental*

Concepts of Metaphysics: World, Finitude, Solitude (Bloomington: Indiana University Press, 1995), part 1, chs 4–5. For an account of "boredom" in Heidegger, also in relation to "anxiety," see Miguel de Beistegui, "Boredom: Between Existence and History: On Heidegger's Pivotal *The Fundamental Concepts of Metaphysics*," *Journal of the British Society for Phenomenology* 31/2 (2000): 145–58.

7 See Heidegger, *Being and Time*, in particular 228–35, 393–6. On "idle talk" (*Gerede*), see also the lecture *Was ist Metaphysik?*, *Wegmarken* (Frankfurt am Main: V. Klostermann, 1967), trans. *What Is Metaphysics?*, in *Pathmarks*, ed. William McNeill (Cambridge: Cambridge University Press, 1998), 82–96.

Part 1, Section 1

1 See Jean Mesnard, "De la 'diversion' au 'divertissement'," in *Mémorial du Premier Congrès International des Études Montaignistes* (Bordeaux: Taffard, 1964), 123–8.

2 "Diversion" for Montaigne is not so much a "strategy" as a "tactic." As Saint-Amand observes, applying Michel de Certeau's distinction in *The Practice of Everyday Life*, to his own reading of Diderot's *Le Neveu de Rameau* (Rameau's Nephew), "a strategy is the result of rational calculation, of a causal and global approach; a tactic, on the other hand, is close to chance: it belongs to the sphere of the random event, the circumstance, the occasion" and "always intervenes on the terrain of others" (see Pierre Saint-Amand, *The Pursuit of Laziness. An Idle Interpretation of the Enlightenment* [Princeton and Oxford: Princeton University Press, 2011], 85).

3 Michel de Montaigne, *Les Essais*, 3 vols, eds. Verdun-Louis Saulnier and Pierre Villey (Paris: Presses Universitaires de France, 2004), vol. III, ch. 4, 835–6, trans. Michael Andrew Screech, *The Complete Essays* (London: Penguin Books, 2003), 941 (henceforth *Essais* followed by indication of the volume, the chapter, and eventually the page number in the French and English editions).

4   See Jean-Charles Darmon, *Philosophies du divertissement. Le Jardin imparfait des modernes* (Paris: Éditions Desjonquères, 2009), 44–9.
5   See Philippe Sellier, *Pascal et Saint Augustin* (Paris: Librairie Armand Colin, 1995), 163–7. For a discussion of Augustine's central claim "ecce distention est vita mea" ("my life is distraction": see *The Confessions*, ed. Carolyn J.-B. Hammond [Cambridge, MA: Harvard University Press, 2016], Book XI, 29.39), behind which there is "an entire philosophy of life as distraction, of distraction as the human condition", see David Marno, *Death Be Not Proud*, ch. 5.
6   See Gilles Deleuze, *Spinoza philosophie pratique* (Paris: Minuit, 1982), 34, trans. Robert Hurley, *Spinoza Practical Philosophy* (San Francisco: City Lights Books, 1988), 22.
7   Ibid.
8   Deleuze, *Spinoza philosophie pratique*, 39, trans. 26.
9   Montaigne's source is Diogenes Laërtius, *Lives and Opinions of Eminent Philosophers*, VI, chs 3 and 5. Diogenes also mentions another famous remark by Antisthenes that certainly did not go unnoticed by Montaigne: "I would rather go mad than feel pleasure."

Part 1, Section 2

1   This is how Voltaire defined this text in a letter to M. Thieriot dated July 14, 1733.
2   For the motif of Pascal's misanthropy, with special reference to Voltaire's reading, see Joseph Harris, *Misanthropy in the Age of Reason. Hating Humanity from Shakespeare to Schiller* (Oxford: Oxford University Press, 2022), 119–24.
3   If further observations were added in the subsequent editions of the *Lettres philosophiques* (in 1739 and 1742), in the last year of his life, 1778, Voltaire was still annotating the edition of the *Pensées* published only a few years earlier by Condorcet: see *Éloge et Pensées de Pascal*, édition établie par Condorcet, annotée par Voltaire, in *Les œuvres complètes de Voltaire*, vol. 80A, ed. Richard Parish (Oxford: Voltaire Foundation, 2008).

4 Voltaire, *Lettres philosophiques*, ed. Frédéric Deloffre (Paris: Gallimard, 1986), Letter 25, XXIII, trans. Prudence L. Steiner, *Philosophical Letters. Or, Letters Regarding the English Nation*, ed. John Leigh (Indianapolis/Cambridge: Hackett Publishing Company, 2007).

5 Voltaire, "Le Mondain", ed. Haydn Trevor Mason, in *Les œuvres complètes de Voltaire*, vol. 16 (Oxford: Voltaire Foundation, 2003), 273–313.

6 Voltaire, "De la frivolité", in *Nouveaux mélanges (1765)*, in *Les œuvres complètes de Voltaire*, vol. 60A, ed. Nicholas Cronk (Oxford: Voltaire Foundation, 2017), 405. See also Sabine Melchior-Bonnet, *Une histoire de la frivolité* (Paris: Librairie Armand Colin, 2013).

7 See Antony McKenna, *De Pascal à Voltaire. Le rôle des Pensées de Pascal dans l'histoire des idées entre 1670 et 1734*, 2 vols (Oxford: Voltaire Foundation, 1990), vol. 2, 895.

Part 1, Section 3

1 See La Bruyère, *Les Caractères ou Les Mœurs de ce siècle*, ed. Antoine Adam (Paris: Gallimard, 1975), "De l'homme," 99, trans. Henri van Laun, *The "Characters" of Jean de La Bruyère* (London: G. Routledge & Sons, 1929).

2 On the context and development of these motifs, and in particular on the controversies around those who might be said to experience *ennui* and what might be done to overcome it, see Scholar, *Émigrés*, 135–7. Scholar discusses the controversy between the godly and the gallants focusing in particular on Madeleine de Scudéry's gallant treatment of *ennui* in her conversation "De l'ennui sans sujet" (On causeless ennui). Scudéry's discussion reveals the fundamentally gendered dimension of these debates. See Madeleine de Scudéry, "Conversation de la magnificence et de la magnanimité" and "Conversation de l'ennui sans sujet," in *Conversations nouvelles sur divers sujets* (Paris: Claude Barbin, 1684), vol. I, 1–118, and vol. II, 457–502, Chloé Hogg, "The King in Trinkets: Madeleine de Scudéry's *Conversations* and the Downsizing of Absolutism," *Journal for Eighteenth-Century Studies* 41 (2018): 355–71,

and Delphine Denis, *La muse galante. Poétique de la conversation dans l'œuvre de Madeleine de Scudéry* (Paris: Éditions Honoré Champion, 1997).

3   See Pascal, *Pensées*, 673 and 644, and Laurent Thirouin, "Le défaut d'une droite méthode," *Littérature classique*, n. 20 (Jan. 1994): 7–21.

4   See Jean Khalfa, "Pascal's Theory of Knowledge," in *The Cambridge Companion to Pascal*, ed. Nicholas Hammond (Cambridge: Cambridge University Press, 2003), 122–42, and Jean-Pierre Cléro, *Pascal* (Paris: Atlande, 2008), 44–5.

5   See Darmon, *Philosophies du divertissement*, 71.

6   "If a man intends to live happy, he must make but few reflections upon life, but often depart, as it were, from himself": Saint-Évremond, *Œuvres en prose*, ed. René Ternois, 4 vols (Paris: Didier, 1962–1969), vol. IV, 12, trans. *The Works of Monsieur de St. Évremond* (London: John Churchill, 1714), vol. I, 43. See Harry T. Barnwell, "Saint-Évremond and Pascal: A Note on the Question of 'Le Divertissement,'" *Studies in Philology* 53, n.1 (Jan. 1956): 35–50.

7   For a historical perspective on the critique of the notion of interiority see Marco Piazza, *Il fantasma dell'interiorità. Breve storia di un concetto controverso* (Milan: Mimesis, 2012).

8   Charles Baudelaire, *Petits poèmes en prose. Le Spleen de Paris* (Paris: Classiques Garnier, 1968), XXIII, "Solitude," trans. Keith Waldrop, *Spleen de Paris. Little Poems in Prose* (Middletown, CT: Wesleyan University Press, 2009).

9   Baudelaire, *Petits poèmes en prose*, XII ("Les foules").

Part 1, Section 4

1   On Voltaire's "polemical stupidity" as a strategic refusal to understand, see, more in general, Robin J. Howells, *Playing Simplicity: Polemical Stupidity in the Writing of the French Enlightenment* (Oxford/Bern: Peter Lang, 2002), which also discusses this strategy with special reference to the *Lettres Philosophiques* and Voltaire's reading of Pascal.

2   See Maine de Biran, *Journal*, ed. Henri Gouhier, 3 vols. (Neuchâtel: Éd. De la Baconnière, 1954–1957), vol. I, 61 (henceforth *Journal*, followed by the volume number and the page).
3   (*Essais*, I, ch. 8).
4   Ibid.
5   See Maine de Biran, *Journal*, II, 299. On religion as a self-discipline technique in Biran, see Marco Piazza, *Il governo di sé. Tempo, corpo e scrittura in Maine de Biran* (Milan: Edizioni Unicopli, 2001).

Part 1, Section 5

1   Jean-Jacques Rousseau, *Les Confessions*, eds. Bernard Gagnebin, Marcel Raymond, and Catherine Koenig (Paris: Gallimard, 1959), Book IX, 496, trans. Christopher Kelly, *The Confessions and Correspondence, Including the Letters to Malesherbes*, eds. Christopher Kelly, Roger D. Masters, and Peter G. Stillman, (Hanover/London: University Press of New England, 1995), 343–4.
2   See Marco Menin, *Il libro mai scritto. La morale sensitiva di Rousseau* (Bologna: Il Mulino, 2013).
3   See Maine de Biran, *Journal*, II, 124–5, and Piazza, *Il governo di sé*, 37–41.
4   See Maine de Biran, *De l'aperception immédiate*, ed. Anne Devarieux (Paris: Librairie Générale Française, 2005), 130–1, trans. Mark Sinclair, *Of Immediate Apperception*, eds. Alessandra Aloisi, Marco Piazza, and Mark Sinclair (London/New York: Bloomsbury, 2020), 74.
5   Giacomo Leopardi, "Il Parini ovvero della gloria," ch. 3, in *Operette morali*, ed. Antonio Prete (Milan: Feltrinelli, Milano, 1992), trans. Giovanni Cecchetti, "Parini on Glory," in *Essays and Dialogues* (Berkeley/Los Angeles/London: University of California Press, 1982).
6   For an analysis of this fragment in relation to the Leibnizian theory of small perceptions see Richard Scholar, *The Je-Ne-Sais-Quoi in Early Modern Europe. Encounters with a Certain Something* (Oxford: Oxford University Press, 2005), 162–73.

7   See Pierre Hadot, *La citadelle intérieure. Introduction aux Pensées de Marc Aurèle* (Paris: Fayard, 1997), 123–44, trans. Michael Chase, *The Inner Citadel: The Meditations of Marcus Aurelius* (Cambridge, MA/London: Harvard University Press, 1998).

Part 1, Section 6

1   See Augustine, *Confessions*, Book X, 10.17.
2   See Alberto Frigo, *L'évidence du Dieu caché. Introduction à la lecture des* Pensées *de Pascal* (Mont-Saint-Aignan: Presses Universitaires de Rouen et du Havre/CNED, 2015), 127–30.

Part 1, Section 7

1   See in particular Giacomo Leopardi, "Dialogo di Torquato Tasso e del suo Genio familiare," in *Operette morali*, trans. "Dialogue between Tasso and His Familiar Spirit," in *Essays and Dialogues*. For the philosophical background to Leopardi's reflections on pleasure and desire, see Antonio Prete, *Il pensiero poetante: saggio su Leopardi* (Milano: Feltrinelli, 2006).
2   Giacomo Leopardi, *Zibaldone*, ed. Giuseppe Pacella, 3 vols (Milano: Garzanti, 1991), vol. 2, 3878, 3921, trans. *Zibaldone: The Notebooks of Leopardi*, eds. Michael Caesar and Franco D'Intino (London: Penguin Classics, 2013). Henceforth *Zibaldone* followed by the page number (as is customary, the page number refers to Leopardi's manuscript).
3   See Leopardi, *Zibaldone*, 650, 165–6.
4   See Pascal, *Pensées*, 112, and Frigo, *L'évidence du Dieu caché*, 126.
5   Leopardi, "Il Parini ovvero della gloria," ch. VI.
6   On the anthropological structure of the "distracted life" in Leopardi and the revival of the motif of the hunt, see Franco D'Intino, *La caduta e il ritorno: cinque movimenti dell'immaginario romantico leopardiano* (Macerata: Quodlibet, 2019), 125–32 and 186–205.

7   See Alessandra Aloisi, "Esperienza del sublime e dinamica del desiderio in Giacomo Leopardi," in *La prospettiva antropologica nel pensiero e nella poesia di Giacomo Leopardi*, ed. Chiara Gaiardoni (Florence: Olschki, 2010), 243–58.

Part 2

1   Montaigne, *Essais*, III, ch. 13, Fr. 1082, Eng. 1228: "Not long ago I came across one of the most learned men in France [...] studying in the corner of his hall which had been partitioned off with tapestries; around him were his menservants making the most disorderly racket. He told me—[C] and Seneca said almost the same of himself—[B] that he found their hubbub useful: it was as though, when he was being battered by that din, he could withdraw and close in on himself so as to meditate, and that those turbulent voices hammered his thought right in. When a student at Padua his study was for so long subject to the clatter of wagons and the tumultuous uproar of the market-place that he had trained himself not merely to ignore the noise but to exploit it in the service of his studies."
2   See Maurizio Ferraris, *Anima e iPad* (Parma: Guanda, 2011).
3   Thomas à Kempis (attributed to), *The Imitation of Christ*, trans. Aloysius Croft and Harold Bolton (New York: Dover Publications, 2012), Book III, ch. 1, 108.
4   See *The Imitation of Christ*, III, ch. 6.
5   See *Angeli. Giudaismo, Islam, Cristianesimo*, eds. Giorgio Agamben and Emanuele Coccia (Vicenza: Neri Pozza, 2009), section "Christianity," ed. E. Coccia, 723: "An angel's intelligence, unlike human intelligence, cannot really turn away from what it thinks: it has either embraced or rejected God's command once and for all. That is why in the face of temptation angels are much weaker than humans, and much more obstinate. The impossibility of distraction acts for both good and evil."

Part 2, Section 1

1. For the afterlives of these Augustinian motifs and examples concerning distraction and the constitutive fragility of human attention in later authors, including Petrarch and John Donne, see Marno, *Death Be Not Proud*.
2. See also Augustin, *The City of God*, ed. William Chase Green (Cambridge, MA: Harvard University Press, 1960), Book XIV, 23.2.
3. Augustine, *On the Free Choice of the Will*, in *Augustine: On the Free Choice of the Will, On Grace and Free Choice, and Other Writings*, ed. Peter King (Cambridge: Cambridge University Press, 2010), Book I, 16.35.
4. Augustine, *The Trinity*, eds. E. Hill and J. E. Rotelle (Brooklyn, NY: New City Press, 1991), Book XII, 12.17, 12.18, 13.20, and 13.21. See also Elémire Zolla, *Storia del fantasticare* (Milan: Bompiani, 1964), 38.
5. See for instance John Donne's funeral sermons: "But when we consider with a religious seriousness the manifold weaknesses of the strongest devotions in time of Prayer, it is a sad consideration. I throw myself downe in my Chamber, and I call in, and invite God, and his Angels thither, and when they are there, I neglect God and his Angles, for the noise of a Flie, for the ratling of a Coach, for the whining of a doore" (John Donne, "Sermon Preached at the Funerals of Sir William Cokayne Knight, Alderman of London, December 12, 1626," in *The Sermons of John Donne*, eds. George Plotter and Evelyn M. Simpson, 10 vols (Berkeley: University of California Press, 1953–62), vol. 7, 264–5.
6. Marcel Proust, *Du côté de chez Swann* (*À la rercherche du temps perdu*, vol. 1), ed. Antoine Compagnon (Paris: Gallimard, 1988), 82, trans. *Swann's Way*, vol. I, 114. The English translation of *À la recherche du temps perdu* is largely based on *In Search of Lost Time*, trans. Charles Kenneth Scott Moncrieff and Terence Kilmartin, revisited by Dennis Joseph Enring, 6 vols (New York: The Modern Library, 2003), with some occasional alterations of my own.

Part 2, Section 2

1. See Étienne B. de Condillac, *Traité des animaux*, ed. Michel Malherbe (Paris: Vrin, 2004), part 1, Conclusion, 142–8. It is no coincidence that in French the expression *chercher la petite bête* (look for the small beast, the insect) is used to condemn the attitude of those who allow themselves to be distracted, in an almost maniacal way, by useless details, paying too much attention to them and losing sight of the overall picture (for the use of this expression, see for instance Proust, *Du côté de chez Swann*, Fr. 209–10, Eng. 298). In *Les Confessions*, Book XII, Fr. 756–7, Eng. 537, Rousseau claims his right to idleness as the right to follow "a fly in all its flying about": "I love to occupy myself by doing trifles, beginning a hundred things and finishing none of them, going and coming as the fancy comes into my head, changing plans at each instant, following a fly in all its flying about, wanting to uproot a rock to see what is under it, undertaking a labor of ten years with ardor, and abandoning it without regret after ten minutes, in sum, musing all day long without order and without sequence, and following only the caprice of the moment in everything." On Rousseau and idleness, see Saint-Amand, *The Pursuit of Laziness*, ch. 3, 51–75.
2. Johannes Colerus, *The Life of Benedict De Spinosa* (London: Printed by D. L. and Sold by Benj. Bragg, at the Raven in Pater-Noster-Row, 1706).
3. See Paolo Cristofolini, *Spinoza per tutti* (Milano: Feltrinelli, 1993), 8.
4. See Spinoza's letter to Blyenburgh on evil (letter XIX) in *The Correspondence of Spinoza*, ed. Abraham Wolf (London: George Allen &; Unwin, 1928), 145–51. For the discussion of this example, see also Deleuze, *Spinoza philosophie pratique*, Fr. 21, Eng. 12.
5. See Baruch Spinoza, *Principles of Cartesian Philosophy*, trans. Harry E. Wedeck (New York: Philosophical Library, 2014), part I, proposition VII, scholium, footnote 5.
6. "I neither wanted nor needed to read further. Immediately, the end of the sentence was like a light of sanctuary poured into my heart; every shadow of doubt melted away" (Augustine, *Confessions*, VIII, 12.29).

7   "I started to ask myself eagerly whether it was common for children to chant such words when they were playing a game of some kind" (Augustine, *Confessions*, VIII, 12.29).
8   See William S. Heckscher, *Art and Literature. Studies in Relationships*, ed. Egon Verheyen (Durham, NC: Duke University Press; Baden-Baden: Verlag Valentin Koerner, 1985), 126–7.
9   And the devil is in the footnotes.

Part 2, Section 3

1   See Pierre Nicole, *Sur l'Évangile du XVIII dimanche d'après la pentecôte*, sections IX–X, in *Continuation des Essais de Morale*, vol. XIII, 117–8. See James, *Pierre Nicole, Jansenist and Humanist*, 112–5.
2   See Margaret A. Boden, *The Creative Mind: Myths and Mechanism* (London/New York: Routledge, 2004), 25.
3   See Henri Poincaré, *Science et méthode* (Paris: Flammarion, 1908), trans. George Bruce Halsted, *Science and Method*, in *The Foundations of Science: Science and Hypothesis, The Value of Science, Science and Method* (Cambridge: Cambridge University Press, 2015), 383–94.
4   Immanuel Kant, *Anthropology from a Pragmatic Point of View*, ed. Robert B. Louden (Cambridge: Cambridge University Press, 2006), I, § 47.
5   See Foucault, *Les aveux de la chair*, ed. Frédéric Gros (Paris: Gallimard, 2018), 136–7, trans. Robert Hurley, *Confessions of the Flesh*, ed. Frédéric Gros (London: Penguin Classics, 2021).
6   See Henri Poincaré, *La valeur de la science* (Paris: Flammarion, 1905), trans. *The Value of Science*, in *The Foundations of Science*, 210–22.
7   See Denis Diderot, "Distraction," in *Encyclopédie*, vol. IV (1754). On distraction and the potentials of the "unfocused mind" in the eighteenth century, with special reference to their literary implications, see Natalie M. Phillips, *Distraction: Problems of Attention in Eighteenth-Century Literature* (Baltimore: The Johns Hopkins University

Press, 2016). For the discussion of Diderot's Encyclopedic entry on "Distraction," see in particular ibid., 106.

8   On the role that the entomological imaginary (made up of bees, worms, mites, termites, and other tiny animals) played, since the early modern period, in the literary figuration of non-conscious psychic processes, especially those related to creativity or invention, see Kate E. Tunstall, "The Early Modern Embodied Mind and the Entomological Imaginary," in *Mind, Body, Motion, Matter: Eighteenth-Century British and French Literary Perspectives*, eds. Mary Helen McMurran and Alison Conway (Toronto: University of Toronto Press, 2016), 202–29.

Part 2, Section 4

1   Paul Chabaneix, *Physiologie cérébrale. Le subconscient chez les artistes, les savants et les écrivains* (Paris: J.B. Baillière & Fils, 1987), 11–2.
2   Pierre-Jean-Georges Cabanis, *Rapports du physique et du moral de l'homme* (Paris: L'imprimerie du Crapelet, 1802), Xème Mémoire ("Du sommeil en particulier"), trans. Margaret Duggan Saidi, *On the Relations between the Physical and Moral Aspects of Man*, ed. George Mora, 2 vols (Baltimore: Johns Hopkins University Press, 1981), vol. 2, 626. These anecdotes are also referred to by Maine de Biran in *Nouvelles considérations sur le sommeil, les songes et le somnambulisme*, in Maine de Biran, *Œuvres*, ed. François Azouvi (Paris: Vrin, 1984–2001), vol. 5, 82–123.
3   See Thomas Hobbes, *Leviathan*, ed. John Charles Addison Gaskin (Oxford: Oxford University Press, 1998), Part I, ch. 3.
4   John Locke, *An Essay Concerning Human Understanding*, ed. Roger S. Woolhouse (London/New York: Penguin, 1997), Book II, ch. 1, § 11 (henceforth *Essay*, followed by the indication of the book, the chapter, and eventually the section).
5   See also *Essay*, II, ch. 27.
6   See Georges Le Roy, *Introduction* to Condillac, *Œuvres philosophiques*, 3 vols (Paris: Presses Universitaires de France, 1947–1951), vol. 1,

XV. On the decisive role of habit in this process see Marco Piazza, *L'antagonista necessario. La filosofia francese dell'abitudine da Montaigne a Deleuze* (Milan: Mimesis, 2015), 85–110.

7   Denis Diderot, *Le Rêve de d'Alembert*, ed. Colas Duflo (Paris: Flammarion, 2002), 156, trans. *D'Alembert's Dream*, in *"Rameau's Nephew" and "D'Alembert's Dream"*, ed. Leonard Tancock (London: Penguin Classics, 1976).

8   See Michael Finn, *Figures of the Pre-Freudian Unconscious from Flaubert to Proust* (Cambridge: Cambridge University Press, 2017), 164–5.

9   Emmanuel Régis, *Préface* à Chabaneix, *Le subconscient*, 5–6.

10 Poincaré, *Science et méthode*, 61–2, trans., 394.

Part 2, Section 5

1   See Nicola Luckhurst, *Science and Structure in Proust's "À la recherche du temps perdu"* (Oxford: Oxford University Press, 2000), 225–44.

2   See Marcel Proust, *Le Temps retrouvé* (*À la rercherche du temps perdu*, vol. 7), ed. Pierre-Edmond Robert (Paris: Gallimard, 1990), 176, trans. *Time Regained*, in *In Search of Lost Time*, vol. VI, 259: "I forced myself to try to discern as quickly as possible the essence of those identical pleasures."

3   See Proust, *Le Temps retrouvé*, Fr. 187, Eng. 276, and Gilles Deleuze, *Proust et les signes* (Paris: Presses Universitaires de France, 1964), trans. Richard Howard, *Proust and Signs. The Complete Text* (Minneapolis: University of Minnesota Press, 2000). For Deleuze's reading of Proust, see Patrick Bray, "Deleuze's *Proust and Signs*: The Literary Partial Object," in *Understanding Deleuze, Understanding Modernism*, eds. Paul Ardoin, Stanley Gontarski, and Laci Mattison (London: Bloomsbury, 2014), 11–20.

4   See Walter Benjamin, "On Some Motifs in Baudelaire," in *Selected Writings*, eds. Michael Jennings et al., 4 vols (Cambridge, MA: Harvard University Press, 1996–2003), vol. IV, 313–55.

5   See Barbara Bucknall, *The Religion of Art in Proust* (Urbana/Chicago/London: University of Illinois Press, 1969), 149–72. For a comparison between Proust and Augustine, see also Angelo Caranfa, "Augustine and Proust on Time," *History of European Ideas* 7, n. 2 (1986): 161–74, and Paul Plass, "Augustine and Proust on Time and Memory," *Soundings: An Interdisciplinary Journal* 73, n. 2/3 (1990): 343–60.

6   Proust, *Le Temps retrouvé*, Fr. 173–5, Eng. 258.

7   Ibid., Fr. 184, Eng. 262.

8   For a discussion of the role of distraction in Proust's novel, see also Michael Wood, *Habits of Distraction*, 36–44. Evelyne Ender, *Architexts of Memory. Literature, Science, and Autobiography* (Ann Arbor: The University of Michigan Press, 2005), 3–4, has rightly pointed out how remembrance, often considered "a triumph of the mind," becomes in Proust an embodied experience: "to respond to the prompting of involuntary cues is to discover a world in which we are alive with sensations, feelings, and human bonds." See in particular ibid., ch. 1, 22–45.

9   See Henri Bergson, *Essai sur les données immédiates de la conscience*, ch. 2, 97–8, and *Le rire*, in *Œuvres*, ed. André Robinet (Paris: Presses Universitaires de France, 1959), ch. 3, 459–60, trans. Cloudesley Brereton and Fred Rothwell, *Laughter: An Essay on the Meaning of the Comic*, ed. Fred Rothwell (New York: Dover Publication, 2013), ch. 3.

10 "Each of us has some routine of living, something that we are used to doing every day, or every so many days, at such and such a time, in such and such a place, occasion, etc. But if this thing or action has become for us [...] so habitual that we do it mechanically, paying no, or almost no attention, very often it will happen that, even shortly afterward, we don't remember if we have done it or not" (Leopardi, *Zibaldone*, 2379–80).

11 Ibid., 1952.

12 See Bergson, *Le rire*, ch. 3, 105, and his lecture "La perception du changement," included in *La pensée et le mouvant*, in *Œuvres*, 1365–92, trans. "The Perception of Change," in *Henri Bergson: Key Writings*, eds.

Keith Ansell Pearson and John Mullarkey (New York: Continuum, 2002), 248–66.

13 See Proust, *Du côté de chez Swann*, Fr. 127, Eng. 180.

14 Friedrich Schiller, *On Grace and Dignity*, in Jane Veronica Curran and Christophe Fricker, *Schiller's "On Grace and Dignity" in Its Cultural Context: Essays and a New Translation* (Suffolk: Boydell & Brewer, 2005), 137.

15 See Giovanni Morelli, *Italian Painters*, trans. Constance Jocelyn Ffoulkes (London: John Murray 1892–1893), on which see especially Edgar Wind, *Art and Anarchy* (Evanston, IL: Northwestern University Press, 1985), 30–47, and Carlo Ginzburg, *Miti, emblemi, spie. Morfologia e storia* (Turin: Einaudi, 1986), 158–209, trans. John and Anne C. Tedeschi, *Clues, Myths, and the Historical Method* (Baltimore: Johns Hopkins University Press, 2013). For the analysis of the connoisseurship method in Proust, see also Mauro Minardi, "Morelli, Berenson, Proust. 'The Art of Connoisseurship'," *Studi di Memofonte* 14 (2015): 211–26.

16 Bergson, *Le rire*, ch. 1, Fr. 399–440, Eng. 25.

17 See Proust, *Du côté de chez Swann*, Fr. 125, Eng. 177.

18 See Marcel Proust, *La Prisonnière* (*À la rercherche du temps perdu*, vol. 5), ed. Pierre-Edmond Robert (Paris: Gallimard, 1989), 80, trans. Charles Kenneth Scott Moncrieff, *The Captive*, in *In Search of Lost Time*, vol. V, 109.

19 Marcel Proust, *Le Côté de Guermantes* (*À la rercherche du temps perdu*, vol. 3), eds. Therry Laget and Birand Rogers (Paris: Gallimard, 1988), 59, trans. *The Guermantes Way*, in *In Search of Lost Time*, vol. III, 80. On deciphering in Proust, see Mariolina Bongiovanni Bertini, *Proust e la teoria del romanzo* (Turin: Bollati Boringhieri, 1996), 150–207.

20 Sigmund Freud, "Recommendations to Physicians Practicing Psychoanalysis," in *The Standard Edition of the Complete Psychological Works of Sigmund Freud* (London: Hogarth Press, 1953–1974), vol. 12 (1911–1913), 109–20.

21 Freud, "Recommendations to Physicians Practicing Psychoanalysis," 111.

22 For the comparison between Proust's and Freud's cognitive method, see Ginzburg, *Clues, Myths, and the Historical Method*, which also shows Freud's debt to Morelli.
23 Freud, "Recommendations to Physicians Practicing Psychoanalysis," 114. As Freud points out, this method also serves a practical purpose: it enables the analyst to economize their attention, which could not be kept up for several hours a day (when an analyst is treating more than one patient in a day, it is difficult to keep in mind all the names, dates, or details which each patient communicates). In this sense, as Freud acknowledges at the beginning of his essay, this technique is suited to his individual constitution, but another physician, differently constituted, might want to adopt a different attitude.
24 Freud, "Recommendations to Physicians Practicing Psychoanalysis," 112.
25 For the difference between "sign" and "symptom" see Jacques Rancière, *L'inconscient esthétique* (Paris: Galilée, 2001), in particular 57–61, trans. Debra Keats and James Swenson, *The Aesthetic Unconscious* (Cambridge: Polity Press, 2009).
26 See Sigmund Freud, *Psychopathology of Everyday Life* (ch. VII), in *The Standard Edition of the Complete Psychological Works of Sigmund Freud*, vol. 6 (1901).

Part 2, Section 6

1 Marcel Proust, *À l'ombre des jeunes filles en fleurs* (*À la rercherche du temps perdu*, vol. 2), ed. Pierre-Louis Rey (Paris: Gallimard, 1988), 285, trans. *Within a Budding Grove*, in *In Search of Lost Time*, vol. II, 404.
2 See Stendhal, *Vie de Henry Brulard*, ed. Béatrice Didier (Paris: Gallimard, 1973), 418, trans. Jean Stewart, *The Life of Henry Brulard* (London: Penguin Classics, 1995).
3 See Miguel de Beistegui, *Proust as Philosopher: The Art of Metaphor* (London and New York: Routledge, 2013), 44–65.

Part 2, Section 7

1. See Proust, *Du côté de chez Swann*, Fr. 269–272, Eng. 387–391.
2. I am freely borrowing this image from Deleuze, *Proust et les signes*, Fr. 218.
3. See Simone Weil, *La pesanteur et la grâce* (Paris: Plon, 1947), 191–200 ("Attention et volonté"), trans. Emma Craufurd, *Gravity and Grace* (London: Routledge and Kegan Paul, 1952), 105–11 ("Attention and Will").
4. See Proust, *À l'ombre des jeunes filles en fleurs*, Fr. 402, Eng. 570.
5. See Proust, *Du côté de chez Swann*, Fr. 269, Eng. 389.
6. See Jacques Rancière, *Politique de la littérature* (Paris: Galilée, 2007), 74–9, trans. Julie Rose, *The Politics of Literature* (Cambridge: Polity Press, 2011), 63–6.
7. See Proust, *Du côté de chez Swann*, Fr. 210, 369, Eng. 300–301, 533.
8. For a comparison of Swann's sterile laziness and the narrator's creative idleness, see Patrick Bray, "Lazy Proust and Literary 'Work,'" *Nottingham French Studies* 55, n. 1 (2016): 18–28.

Part 2, Section 8

1. See Proust, *Le Temps retrouvé*, Fr. 186, Eng. 275.

Part 3

1. See Kant, *Anthropology from a Pragmatic Point of View*, I, § 47. In a letter to Vieusseux (March 4, 1826) Leopardi apologized for his absent-mindedness, justifying it as a "vice" that had become "incorrigible and desperate": see Giacomo Leopardi, *Epistolario*, eds. Franco Brioschi and Patrizia Landi (Turin: Bollati, 1998).

2   See Jean de La Bruyère, section 99 in the chapter "De l'homme," in *Les Caractères ou Les Moeurs de ce siècle*, ed. Antoine Adam (Paris: Gallimard, 1975), trans. Jean Stewart, *Characters* (Baltimore: Penguin, 1970).
3   Diderot, "Distraction," in *Encyclopédie*, vol. IV.

Part 3, Section 1

1   See Huntington Williams, *Rousseau and Romantic Autobiography* (Oxford: Oxford University Press, 1983), 9–10, and the entries "Rêverie" and "Rêver" in *Dictionnaire historique de la langue française*, 3 vols (Paris: Le Robert, Paris, 1998), vol. III, and *Dictionnaire des étymologies obscures*, ed. Pierre Guiraud (Paris: Payot, 1982).
2   See *Oxford English Dictionary* (Oxford: Oxford University Press, 2010), entries "Daydream" and "Mind-wandering."
3   See Remo Bodei, *Immaginare altre vite. Realtà, progetti, desideri* (Milan: Feltrinelli, 2013), 34–41. In some respects, the Italian term *fantasticheria* seems to have some important similarities with what Freud calls daydreams (*Tagträume*). For a discussion of the different meanings and functions of "daydreams" in Freud in relation to "night-dreams" (*Nachtträume*), see Rachel Bowlby, "The Other Day: The Interpretation of Daydreams," in *Freudian Mythologies. Greek Tragedy and Modern Identities* (Oxford: Oxford University Press, 2007), 101–23. As Bowlby shows, daydreams can sometimes be associated by Freud with the "day's residues" (*Tagesresten*)—something from the previous day that, being free of associations because of its insignificance, go into the making of dreams (unimportant thoughts or activities, meaningless details or impressions). At the same time, daydreams can also denote something very similar to what Freud will also call "fantasies" or "phantasies" (*Phantasien*). In this case, daydreams are not what contributes to the making of dreams, but they resemble night-dreams. Like night-dreams, daydreams or phantasies are "narratives which lead to satisfaction by representing the fulfillment of wishes" (Bowlby, 107). However, unlike dreams, and more similarly to *fantasticherie*, daydreams or phantasies are "more straightforward, unified, and

unidirectional stories of wish-fulfillment" (110). As Freud points out, unlike dreams, daydreams or phantasies are never experienced as hallucinations, they imply self-awareness, and the daydreamer has some control over them. Furthermore, according to Freud, phantasies or daydreams are usually gendered or reproduce gender clichés.

4 Diderot, "Distraction."
5 For the specificity of reverie and its relation to dream, see also Gaston Bachelard, *La poétique de la rêverie* (Paris: Presses Universitaires de France, 1960), trans. Daniel S. Russell, *The Poetics of Reverie: Childhood, Language and the Cosmos* (Boston, MA: Beacon, 1971), and *Le droit de rêver* (Paris: Presses Universitaires de France, 1970), trans. James Amery Underwood, *The Right to Dream* (Dallas: Dallas Institute of Humanities and Culture, 1988).
6 Giacomo Leopardi, *Discorso di un italiano intorno alla poesia romantica*, ed. Ottavio Besomi (Bellinzona: Edizioni Casagrande, 1998), 10, trans. Gabrielle Sims and Fabio Camilletti, *Leopardi's Discourse on Romantic Poetry*, in Fabio Camilletti, *Classicism and Romanticism in Italian Literature* (London: Pickering & Chatto, 2013).
7 See Henri Bergson, *L'énergie spirituelle*, in *Œuvres*, 896, trans. Herbert Wildon Carr, *Mind-Energy: Lectures and Essays* (London: Macmillan, 1920), 132.
8 See Hippolyte Taine, *De l'intelligence* (Paris: Librairie Hachette, 1870), vol. 1, 424 and 439, trans. T. D. Haye and revised by the author, *On Intelligence* (London: Savill, Edwards and Co., Printers, 1871).
9 For the sensation of déja vu, see Remo Bodei, *La sensation du déjà vu* (Paris: Seuil, 2007).

Part 3, Section 2

1 See Jean Piaget, *La formation du symbole chez l'enfant: imitation, jeu et rêve, image et représentation* (Paris: Delachaux et Niestlé, 1945), trans. *Play, Dreams and Imitation in Childhood* (New York: W.W. Norton & Co., 1962).
2 See Bachelard, *La poétique de la rêverie*, 84–123.
3 See Marcel Raymond, *Romantisme et rêverie* (Paris: José Corti, 1978).

4   George Sand, *Histoire de ma vie* (Paris: Gallimard, 2004), part 2, ch. XVI, trans. *Story of My Life: The Autobiography of George Sand*, ed. Thelma Jurgrau (Albany, N.Y.: State University of New York Press, 1991), 485.
5   See Heidegger, *Being and Time*, part 1, division 1, III.
6   Proust, *Du côté de chez Swann*, Fr. 111–2, Eng. 155–6.
7   Gustave Flaubert, *Madame Bovary* (Paris: Gallimard, 2001), part 1, ch. 6, 85, trans. Margaret Maudlon, *Madame Bovary: Provincial Manners* (Oxford: Oxford University Press, 2020), 199. For a reading of this passage, see Rancière, *Politique de la littérature*, Fr. 70–2, Eng. 57–8.
8   Gérard Genette, "Silences de Flaubert," in *Figures I* (Paris: Seuil, 1966), 223–43, trans. Alan Sheridan, "Flaubert's Silences," in *Figures of Literary Discourse* (Oxford: Basic Blackwell Publisher, 1982), 183–202.
9   Gustave Flaubert, *La Tentation de saint Antoine*, version of 1849 (Paris: Conard, 1924), 418. The "correspondences" between the first version of *La Tentation* and *Madame Bovary* (correspondences later discussed also by Genette and Rancière) had been highlighted first by Charles Baudelaire, "*Madame Bovary* par Gustave Flaubert," in *L'art romantique*, ed. Blaise Allan (Lausanne: La Guilde du Livre, 1950), 330–40.
10 Gustave Flaubert, *Lettres à Louise Colet: Correspondance 1846–1851* (Lausanne: Éditions Rencontre, 1964), letter of May 26, 1853.
11 Thomas De Quincey, *The Last Days of Immanuel Kant and Other Writings* (Edinburgh: Adam and Charles Black, 1862), 115.

Part 3, Section 3

1   Rousseau, *Les Confessions*, Book IV, Fr. 215, Eng. 136. On the fatigue of thinking, overcome in reverie, see also *Les Confessions*, Book III, Fr. 159, Eng. 95, and Jean-Jacques Rousseau, *Les Rêveries du promeneur solitaire*, ed. Érik Leborgne (Paris: Flammarion, 1997), trans. Russell

Goulbourne, *Reveries of the Solitary Walker* (Oxford: Oxford University Press, 2022), seventh walk.

2 On the relationship between travel, walking, and reverie in Rousseau, see in particular Barbara Carnevali, "L''eterno viaggiatore'. Jean-Jacques Rousseau," in *I viaggi dei filosofi*, eds. Maria Bettetini and Stefano Poggi (Milan: Cortina, 2010), 135–58.

3 On Leopardi's travels see Attilio Brilli, *In viaggio con Leopardi* (Bologna: Il Mulino, 2000).

4 Proust, *À l'ombre des jeunes filles en fleurs*, Fr. 213, Eng. 302. See also ibid., Fr. 225, Eng. 319. On travel by automobile see Marcel Proust, "Impressions de route en automobile," in *Écrits sur l'art*, 249–55.

5 Rousseau, *Les Rêveries*, fifth walk, Fr. 104, Eng. 56.

6 Bergson, *Essai sur les données immédiates*, ch. 1, Fr. 11, Eng. 14.

7 Rousseau, *Les Rêveries*, fifth walk, Fr. 104, Eng. 56–7. Tehching Hsieh, a Taiwanese-born American artist, seems to have put Rousseau's extremism to the test when in 1978 he had himself locked up for 365 days—without books, TV, radio, or other forms of entertainment—in a wooden cage for his *One Year Performance (Cage Piece)*.

8 See Saint-Amand, *The Pursuit of Laziness*, 65–73.

9 See Leopardi, "Dialogo di Torquato Tasso e del suo Genio familiare." I would like to thank Emanuela Tandello, Olmo Calzolari, and Caroline Warman for the opportunity to discuss this *operetta* together during a seminar organized by LEO (Leopardi Studies at Oxford).

10 Xavier de Maistre, *Voyage autour de ma chambre* (Paris: Flammarion, 2003), ch. 42, 132–3, trans. Stephen Sartarelli, *Voyage around My Room: Selected Works of Xavier de Maistre* (New York: New Directions, 1994), 115 (henceforth *Voyage* followed by the indication of the chapter and page numbers in the French and English editions). For a reading of these pages by Xavier de Maistre, also in relation to Maine de Biran and Stendhal, see Marco Piazza, "Fra camere e torri, in vista di se stessi. Maine de Biran, Xavier de Maistre e Henri Beyle," in *I viaggi dei filosofi*, 159–76.

11   Jacques Rancière, *Aisthesis. Scènes du régime esthétique de l'art* (Paris: Galilée, 2011), 67, trans. Zakir Paul, *Aisthesis. Scenes from the Aesthetic Regime of Art* (London, New York: Verso, 2013), 45.
12   See Rousseau, *Les Rêveries*, second walk, Fr. 46, Eng. 12, and fifth walk, Fr. 103–104, Eng. 56.
13   Giacomo Leopardi, Preambolo alla ristampa delle *Annotazioni* nel "Nuovo Ricoglitore" di Milan, Settembre 1825, in *Poesie e prose*, ed. Mario Andrea Rigoni (Milan: Mondadori, 1987), vol. 1, 165.
14   Rousseau, *Les Confessions*, Book IV, Fr. 215–6, Eng. 136.
15   See Rousseau, *Les Rêveries*, seventh walk, Fr. 136, Eng. 80.
16   Baudelaire, *Petits poèmes en prose*, XII ("Les foules").

Part 3, Section 4

1   See Condillac, *Traité des animaux*, part 2, ch. 5, 164.
2   On the so-called double law of habit and its implications see in particular Marco Piazza, *Creature dell'abitudine. Abito, costume, seconda natura da Aristotele alle scienze cognitive* (Bologna: Il Mulino, 2018), 171–200.
3   Samuel Butler, *Life and Habit* (London: Jonathan Cape, 1878), ch. I.
4   See Italo Svevo, *La coscienza di Zeno* (Milan: Feltrinelli, 1993), ch. 5, trans. Beryl de Zoete, *Confessions of Zeno* (London: Putnam, 1930), 102.
5   See Franco D'Intino, "Il monaco indiavolato. Lo *Zibaldone* e la tentazione faustiana di Leopardi," in *Lo* Zibaldone *cento anni dopo. Composizione, edizioni, temi*, ed. Rolando Garbuglia, 2 vols (Florence: Olschki, 2001), vol. 2, 467–523.

Part 3, Section 5

1   Freud, *Psychopathology of Everyday Life*, ch. VII.
2   See Bergson, *Essai sur les données immédiates*, ch. 3, Fr. 120–1, Eng. 166–7.

3   See La Bruyère, *Les Caractères*, section 99 in the chapter "De l'homme."
4   For the example of the orchestra conductor, see Pierre Janet, *L'automatisme psychologique* (Paris: Félix Alcan, 1889), 195.
5   See Bergson, *Essai sur les données immédiates*, ch. 3, Fr. 125, Eng. 171.

Part 3, Section 6

1   Janet, *L'automatisme psychologique*, 190–9.
2   See Biran, *Journal*, I, 31, and II, 21. Janet quotes him in *L'automatisme psychologique*, 162.
3   Leopardi, *Epistolario*, Letter to Vieusseux, March 4, 1826. The English is in the original.
4   Maine de Biran, *Nouvelles considérations sur le sommeil, les songes et le somnambulisme*, 114.
5   See Maine de Biran, *De l'aperception immédiate*, Fr. 205, Eng. 124.
6   Alessandro Manzoni, *I promessi sposi* (Milan: Feltrinelli, 2003), ch. IX, trans. *The Betrothed* (London: Lambert & Co., 1856), 105. According to Zolla, *Storia del fantasticare*, 160, Gertrude is the Italian version of Julien Sorel, Emma Bovary, and Anna Karenina. For Manzoni's portrayal of Gertrude, see Fabio Camilletti, "Gertrude e il Nome del Padre," *Italian Studies* 71, n. 1 (February 2016): 82–97.
7   Proust, *À l'ombre des jeunes filles en fleurs*, Fr. 361, Eng. 512.
8   On Archimedes's distraction, which would cause him to forget to eat or even to stumble to the ground, see Plutarch, *Parallel Lives*, who also recounts his murder. For a record of the sources and illustrations concerning Archimedes's death, see the website on Archimedes hosted by NYU: https://www.math.nyu.edu/~crorres/Archimedes/Death/DeathIllus.html.
9   Bergson, *Essai sur les données immédiates*, ch. 2, Fr. 94–5, Eng. 136.
10 Proust, "Sur la lecture," in *Écrits sur l'art*, 199, trans. Damion Searls, *On Reading* (London: Hesperus Press Limited, 2011), 65.
11 Rather than as function of consciousness, attention should be understood as a function of memory. As Leibniz suggests: "All

attention requires memory, and often when we are not admonished, so to speak, and advised to attend to some of our own present perceptions, we let them pass without reflection and even without being noticed; but if someone calls our attention to them immediately afterwards and makes us notice, for example, some noise which was just heard, we remember it and are conscious of having had at the time some feeling of it. Thus they were perceptions of which we were not immediately conscious" (Gottfried Wilhelm Leibniz, *New Essays Concerning Human Understanding*, in *Selections*, ed. Philip Paul Wiener [New York: Charles Scribner's Sons, 1951], 374–5).

Part 3, Section 7

1   See Michel Foucault, *Histoire de la folie à l'âge classique* (Paris: Gallimard, 1972), trans. Jean Khalfa and Jonathan Murphy, *History of Madness* (London: Routledge, 2006), part II, ch. 2.
2   *Encyclopédie*, vol. 6 (1756), entry "folie" (morale), where, however, we also find the distinction between *folies physiques* (physical follies) and *folies morales* (moral follies).
3   Voltaire, *Dictionnaire philosophique*, 2 vols, in *Œuvres complètes de Voltaire*, vol. 35:36, ed. Christiane Mervaud (Oxford: Voltaire Foundation, 1994), "folie," trans. John Fletcher, *A Pocket Philosophical Dictionary*, ed. Nicholas Cronk (Oxford: Oxford University Press, 2011), 143.
4   After all, as Lacan ironically observed while commenting on Descartes, with a remark in which resonates Pascal, a king really convinced of being a king would be no less mad than the madman who thought he was a king. See Jacques Lacan, "Propos sur la causalité psychique," in *Écrits*, vol. 1 (Paris: Seuil, 1966), trans. Bruce Fink, Héloïse Fink, and Russell Grigg, *Ecrits: The First Complete Edition in English* (New York, London: W. W. Norton & Co., 2006), and Pascal, *Pensées*, 31: "Men are so necessarily mad that it would be another twist of madness not to be mad."

5   In this sense it is also interesting to mention the expression "It [Bethlem] was a Hospital for distracted people," used by James Howell, *Londinopolis; An Historical Discourse or Perlustraction of the City of London* (1657): see *Oxford English Dictionary* (Oxford: Oxford University Press, 2010), entry "Distracted." See also Carol Thomas Neely, *Distracted Subjects. Madness and Gender in Shakespeare and Early Modern Culture* (Ithaca, NY: Cornell University Press, 2004), which shows how in the early modern period, distraction mainly denoted a state of madness.

6   See Locke, *Essay*, II, ch. 11, § 17.

7   B89. The numeration of the fragment is that of the sixth edition of Diels-Kranz, *Fragmente der Vorsokratiker*, 3 vols (Berlin, 1951). The translation is Charles Kahn's: *The Art and Thought of Heraclitus* (Cambridge: Cambridge University Press, 1979), 31.

8   See for instance the entry "folie" in Voltaire's *Dictionnaire philosophique*, where dreams are defined as a form of "passing madness," and the entry "rêve" (section *métaphysique*) in Diderot and d'Alembert's *Encyclopédie*, where dreams are compared to delirium. In classical French, at least until the seventeenth and eighteenth centuries, one of the main meanings of the terms *rêver* and *rêverie* was precisely that of delirium (see for instance *Dictionnaire historique de la langue française*, vol. III).

9   Diderot, "Distraction," and *Le Neveu de Rameau* (Paris: Gallimard, 1972), 31.

10 See Foucault, *Histoire de la folie à l'âge classique*, preface to the first edition (1960), Eng. 164.

11 See La Bruyère, *Les Caractères*, section 99 in the chapter "De l'homme."

12 See Bergson, *Le rire*, ch. 1, Fr. 392, Eng. 15, and Roland Barthes, *Essais critiques* (Paris: Seuil, 1964), 233, trans. Richard Howard, *Critical Essays* (Evanston, IL.: Northwestern University Press, 1972), 221–38.

13 For the overlap between distraction and madness, with special reference to La Bruyère's Ménalque, see in particular the insightful analysis of Paul North, *The Problem of Distraction*, ch. 2.

Part 3, Section 8

1. *Encyclopédie*, vol. 6 (1756), entry "Folie" (morale).
2. Ibid.
3. For the "alertness attentional regime," see Dominique Boullier, "Composition médiatique d'un monde commun à partir du pluralisme des régimes d'attention," in *Conflit des interprétations dans la société d'information*, eds. Pierre-Antoine Chardel, Cédric Gossart, and Bernard Reber (Paris: Hermès, 2012), 41–57.
4. See Bergson, *Le rire*, ch. 3, Fr. 475–6, Eng. 122–3.
5. Ibid. As Bergson points out, this inversion of common sense, which distraction consists in, could be called madness, were it not for the fact that the latter is a disease, whereas distraction is not.
6. See Gilles Deleuze, *Différence et répétition* (Paris: Presses Universitaires de France, 1968), 169–217, trans. Paul Patton, *Difference and Repetition* (New York: Columbia University Press, 1995), 129–67.
7. See Maine de Biran, *Nouvelles considérations*, 115 and Taine, *De l'intelligence*, 412.
8. See Jacques Rancière, *Le spectateur émancipé* (Paris: La Fabrique, 2008), 19–23, trans. Gregory Elliott, *The Emancipated Spectator* (London: Verso, 2011). On the "emancipatory distraction" that brings out a "dissensual look," see Citton, *Pour une écologie de l'attention*, 170.
9. In the street, lost in thought, Ménalque regularly fails to bow when a prince passes by. Mistaken for a bishop, a lackey is called "my lord," while a lawyer in a robe receives the flirtatious salutation of "miss." Following an exchange of letters, a hay supplier receives an obsequious message addressed to a duke, who is instead given an order to send the agreed provision as soon as possible. Again, mistaken for a prayer book, a slipper is brought to church, producing a disjunction between certain objects and their socially shared meaning.
10. For the analysis of these pages by La Bruyère, I refer to Marc Escola, *La Bruyère I, Brèves questions d'herméneutique* (Paris: Honoré Champion,

2001), ch. VI. Escola also convincingly discusses how distraction is performed within the text and by the text itself, which becomes a sort of "textual *analogon*" of Ménalque's distraction (337–8).

11 Bergson, "La perception du changement," Fr. 1370, Eng. 251.
12 See Water Benjamin, "The Work of Art and Its Technological Reproduction," in *Illuminations*, ed. Hannah Arendt, trans. Harry Zohn (New York: Harcourt, Brace & World, 1968).
13 Bergson, *Le rire*, Fr. 461, Eng. 105.
14 Deleuze, *Différence et répétition*, Fr. 181, Eng. 139.

Part 3, Section 9

1 See Michel Foucault, *Maladie mentale et psychologie* (Paris: Presses Universitaires de France, 1954), 71–5, trans. Alan Sheridan, *Mental Illness and Psychology* (Berkeley/Los Angeles/London: University of California, 2008), 60–4.
2 Citton, *Pour une écologie de l'attention*.
3 See Baudelaire, *Le Spleen de Paris*, XLIV ("La soupe et les nuages").
4 See Foucault, *Maladie mentale et psychologie*, Fr. 80, Eng. 6, and *Histoire de la folie à l'âge classique*, part I, ch. 1.
5 On the "amusement industry" see Theodor W. Adorno and Max Horkheimer, *Dialectics of the Enlightenment: Philosophical Fragments*, ed. Gunzelin Schmid Noerr, trans. Edmund Jephcott. (Stanford: Stanford University Press, 2002), for which "entertainment is the prolongation of work under later capitalism" (ibid., 109). For the difference between *distraction* and *entertainment*, see Niklas Luhmann, *The Reality of the Mass Media*, trans. Kathleen Cross (Stanford: Stanford University Press, 2000) and Dork Zabunyan, Postface to Zoe Beloff, *Techniques de la distraction*, ed. Paul Sztulman and Dork Zabunyan (Dijon: Les presses du réel; Paris: ArTeC, 2019), 122–3, which adopts a perspective inspired by Kracauer, Benjamin, and Rancière.

Conclusion

1. See Bergson, *Le rire*, ch. 1, Fr. 395–6, Eng. 19.
2. Ibid., Fr. 472 and 483, Eng. 118 and 134.
3. For the history and meaning of this anecdote concerning Thales of Miletus, originally found in Plato's *Theaetetus*, see Hans Blumenberg, *The Laughter of the Thracian Woman: A Protohistory of Theory*, trans. Spencer Hawkins (New York: Bloomsbury, 2015).
4. See Bergson, *Le rire*, ch. 1, Fr. 388, Eng. 10. For the idea of man as *animale risibile*, see Giacomo Leopardi, "Elogio degli uccelli," in *Operette morali*, trans. "Panegiric of Birds," in *Essays and Dialogues*. The definition of man as a "laughing animal" was proposed by Aristotle, who called humans "the only creatures that laugh" (see Aristotle, *Parts of Animals*, book III, 673 a, in *Parts of Animals—Movement of Animals—Progression of Animals*, trans. Arthur Leslie Peck and Edward Seymour Forster [Cambridge, MA: Harvard University Press, 1937], 281). This Aristotelian definition had already been contested by Jean-François Regnard in his comedy *Démocrite*, where Democritus calls man a "ridiculous animal" [*animal ridicule*]. For a discussion of this motif, which "retains laughter as a constituent element of mankind but utterly inverts its direction," see Harris, *Misanthropy in the Age of Reason*, ch. 3, 86–115. Harris shows how, in the early modern period, "the laughter that for Aristotelians had marked mankind's superiority over the animal world is now—humiliatingly—turned back against mankind itself" (86) and acquires a misanthropic connotation. In its corrective aspect, however, laughter does not spare the misanthropist, who is laughed at as much as he laughs at other people.
5. Ibid., ch. 1, Fr. 392, Eng. 15.
6. Ibid., ch. 3, Fr. 480–1, Eng. 130–3.

Bibliography

Adorno, T. W., and Horkheimer, M., *Dialectics of the Enlightenment: Philosophical Fragments*, ed. G. S. Noerr; trans. E. Jephcott., Stanford: Stanford University Press, 2002.

Agamben, G., *Stanze. La parola e il fantasma nella cultura occidentale*, Turin: Einaudi, 1977; trans. R. L. Martinez, *Stanzas: Word and Phantasm in Western Culture*, Minneapolis/London: University of Minnesota Press, 1993.

Agamben, G., "Su ciò che possiamo non fare," in *Nudità*, Rome: Nottetempo, 2009; trans. D. Kishik and S. Pedatella, "On What We Can Not Do," in *Nudities*, Stanford: Stanford University Press, 2011.

Agamben, G., and Coccia, E., eds., *Angeli. Giudaismo, Islam, Cristianesimo*, Vicenza: Neri Pozza, 2009.

Aloisi, A., "Esperienza del sublime e dinamica del desiderio in Giacomo Leopardi," in *La prospettiva antropologica nel pensiero e nella poesia di Giacomo Leopardi*, ed. C. Gaiardoni, Florence: Olschki, 2010, 243–58.

Aristotle, *Parts of Animals—Movement of Animals—Progression of Animals*, trans. A. L. Peck and E. S. Forster, Cambridge, MA: Harvard University Press, 1937.

Arpe, E. S., "Il compito politico della distrazione," *Intersezioni* XLII, n. 2 (August 2022): 213–27.

Augustine of Hippo, *The City of God*, ed. W. C. Green, Cambridge, MA: Harvard University Press, 1960.

Augustine of Hippo, *The Trinity*, eds. E. Hill and J. E. Rotelle, Brooklyn, NY: New City Press, 1991.

Augustine of Hippo, *On the Free Choice of the Will*, in *On the Free Choice of the Will, On Grace and Free Choice, and Other Writings*, ed. P. King, Cambridge: Cambridge University Press, 2010.

Augustine of Hippo, *The Confessions*, ed. C. J.-B. Hammond, Cambridge, MA: Harvard University Press, 2016.

Bachelard, G., *La poétique de la rêverie*, Paris: Presses Universitaires de France, 1960; trans. D. S. Russell, *The Poetics of Reverie: Childhood, Language and the Cosmos*, Boston, MA: Beacon, 1971.

Bachelard, G., *Le droit de rêver*, Paris: Presses Universitaires de France, 1970; trans. J. A. Underwood, *The Right to Dream*, Dallas: Dallas Institute of Humanities and Culture, 1988.

Barnwell, H. T., "Saint-Évremond and Pascal: A Note on the Question of 'Le Divertissement," *Studies in Philology* 53, n. 1 (Jan. 1956): 35–50.

Barthes, R., *Le plaisir du texte*, Paris: Seuil, 1973; trans. R. Miller, *The Pleasure of the Text*, New York: Hill and Wang, 1975.

Baudelaire, C., "*Madame Bovary* par Gustave Flaubert," in *L'art romantique*, ed. B. Allan, Lausanne: La Guilde du Livre, 1950, 330–40.

Baudelaire, C., *Petits poèmes en prose. Le Spleen de Paris*, Paris: Classiques Garnier, 1968; trans. K. Waldrop, *Spleen de Paris. Little Poems in Prose*, Middletown, CT: Wesleyan University Press, 2009.

Beistegui, M. de, "Boredom: Between Existence and History: On Heidegger's Pivotal *The Fundamental Concepts of Metaphysics*," *Journal of the British Society for Phenomenology*, 31/2 (2000): 145–58.

Beistegui, M. de, *Proust as Philosopher: The Art of Metaphor*, London/New York: Routledge, 2013.

Beloff, B., *Techniques de la distraction*, eds. P. Sztulman and D. Zabunyan, Dijon: Les presses du réel; Paris: ArTeC, 2019.

Benjamin, W., "The Work of Art and Its Technological Reproduction," in *Illuminations*, trans. H. Zohn, ed. H. Arendt, New York: Harcourt, Brace & World, 1968.

Benjamin, W., *Selected Writings*, eds. M. Jennings et al., 4 vols, Cambridge, MA: Harvard University Press, 1996–2003.

Bergson, H., *L'énergie spirituelle*, in *Œuvres*, ed. A. Robinet, Paris: Presses Universitaires de France, 1959; trans. H. W. Carr, *Mind-Energy: Lectures and Essays*, London: Macmillan, 1920.

Bergson, H., *L'Évolution créatrice*, Paris: Presses Universitaires de France, 1948; trans. A. Mitchell, *Creative Evolution*, London: Electric Book, 2001.

Bergson, H., "La perception du changement," in *La pensée et le mouvant*, in *Œuvres*, ed. A. Robinet, Paris: Presses Universitaires de France, 1959; trans. "The Perception of Change," in *Henri Bergson: Key Writings*, eds. K. A. Pearson and J. Mullarkey, New York: Continuum 2002, 248–66.

Bergson, H., *Essai sur les données immédiates de la conscience*, ed. F. Worms, Paris: Presses Universitaires de France, 2013; trans. F. L. Pogson, *Time and Free Will: An Essay on the Immediate Data of Consciousness*, New York: Dover Publication, 2012.

Bergson, H., *Le rire*, in *Œuvres*, ed. A. Robinet, Paris : Presses Univesitaires de France, 1959; trans. C. Brereton and F. Rothwell, *Laughter: An Essay on the Meaning of the Comic*, ed. F. Rothwell, New York: Dover Publication, 2013.

Blumenberg, H., *The Laughter of the Thracian Woman: A Protohistory of Theory*, trans. S. Hawkins, New York: Bloomsbury, 2015.

Bodei, R. *La sensation du déjà vu*, Paris: Seuil, 2007.

Bodei, R. *Immaginare altre vite. Realtà, progetti, desideri*, Milan: Feltrinelli, 2013.

Boden, M. A., *The Creative Mind: Myths and Mechanism*, London/New York: Routledge, 2004.

Bongiovanni Bertini, M., *Proust e la teoria del romanzo*, Turin: Bollati Boringhieri, 1996.

Boullier, D., "Composition médiatique d'un monde commun à partir du pluralisme des régimes d'attention," in *Conflit des interprétations dans la société d'information*, eds. P.-A. Chardel, C. Gossart, and B. Reber, Paris: Hermès, 2012, 41–57.

Bowlby, R., "The Other Day: The Interpretation of Daydreams," in *Freudian Mythologies. Greek Tragedy and Modern Identities*, Oxford: Oxford University Press, 2007, 101–23.

Bray, P., "Deleuze's *Proust and Signs*: The Literary Partial Object," in *Understanding Deleuze, Understanding Modernism*, eds. P. Ardoin, S. Gontarski, and L. Mattison, London: Bloomsbury, 2014.

Bray, P., "Lazy Proust and Literary 'Work'," *Nottingham French Studies* 55, n. 1 (2016): 18–28.

Brilli, A., *In viaggio con Leopardi*, Bologna: Il Mulino, 2000.

Brun, J., *La philosophie de Pascal*, Paris: Presses Universitaires de France, 1992.

Bucknall, B., *The Religion of Art in Proust*, Urbana/Chicago/London: University of Illinois Press, 1969.

Burton, R., *The Anatomy of Melancholy*, eds. T. C. Faulkner, N. K. Kiessling, and R. L. Blair, Oxford: Oxford University Press, 1989.

Butler, S., *Life and Habit*, London: Jonathan Cape, 1878.
Cabanis, P.-J.-G., *Rapports du physique et du moral de l'homme*, Paris : L'imprimerie du Crapelet, 1802; trans. M. D. Saidi, *On the Relations between the Physical and Moral Aspects of Man*, ed. G. Mora, 2 vols, Baltimore: Johns Hopkins University Press, 1981.
Camilletti, F., "Gertrude e il Nome del Padre," *Italian Studies* 71, n. 1 (February 2016): 82–97.
Campo, E., *Attention and Its Crisis in Digital Society*, trans. I. Richard, New York: Routledge, 2022.
Caranfa, A., "Augustine and Proust on Time," *History of European Ideas* 7, n. 2 (1986): 161–74.
Carboni, M., *La mosca di Dreyer. L'opera della contingenza nelle arti*, Milan: Jaka Books, 2007.
Carnevali, B., "L''eterno viaggiatore'. Jean-Jacques Rousseau," in *I viaggi dei filosofi*, eds. M. Bettetini and S. Poggi, Milan: Cortina, 2010, 135–58.
Carraud, V., *Pascal et la philosophie*, Paris: Presses Universitaires de France, 1992.
Chabaneix, P., *Physiologie cérébrale. Le subconscient chez les artistes, les savants et les écrivains*, Paris: J.B. Baillière & Fils, 1987.
Citton, Y., "Économie de l'attention et nouvelles exploitations numériques," *Multitudes* 3, 54 (2013): 163–75.
Citton, Y., ed., *L'économie de l'attention*, Paris : La Découverte, 2014.
Citton, Y., "Attention collective et vigilance médiatique," *Intellecta. Revue de l'Association pour la Recherche Cognitive* 66/2 (2016): 161–80.
Citton, Y., *Pour une écologie de l'attention*, Paris : Seuil, 2014; trans. B. Norman, *The Ecology of Attention*, Cambridge: Polity Press, 2016.
Cléro, J.-P., *Pascal*, Paris: Atlande, 2008.
Colerus, J., *The Life of Benedict De Spinoza*, London: Printed by D. L. and Sold by Benj. Bragg, at the Raven in Pater-Noster-Row, 1706.
Condillac, E. B. de, *Œuvres philosophiques*, 3 vols, Paris: Presses Universitaires de France, 1947–1951.
Condillac, E. B. de, *Traité des animaux*, ed. M. Malherbe, Paris: Vrin, 2004.
Condorcet, N. de, ed., *Éloge et Pensées de Pascal*, édition annotée par Voltaire, in *Les œuvres complètes de Voltaire*, vol. 80A, ed. R. Parish, Oxford : Voltaire Foundation, 2008.

Crary, J., *Techniques of the Observer. On Vision and Modernity in the Nineteenth Century*, Cambridge, MA: MIT Press, 1990.

Crary, J., *Suspensions of Perception: Attention, Perception, and Modern Culture*, Cambridge, MA: MIT Press, 2001.

Crary, J., *24/7. Late Capitalism and the End of Sleep*, New York: Verso, 2013.

Cristofolini, P., *Spinoza per tutti*, Milan: Feltrinelli, 1993.

Darmon, J.-C., *Philosophies du divertissement. Le Jardin imparfait des modernes*, Paris: Éditions Desjonquères, 2009.

Deleuze, G., *Spinoza philosophie pratique*, Paris: Les Éditions de Minuit, 1982; trans. R. Hurley, *Spinoza Practical Philosophy*, San Francisco: City Lights Books, 1988.

Deleuze, G., *Le bergsonisme*, Paris: Presses Universitaires de France, 1966; trans. H. Tomlinson and B. Habberjam, *Bergsonism*, New York: Zone Books, 1990.

Deleuze, G., *Différence et répétition*, Paris: Presses Universitaires de France, 1968; trans. P. Patton, *Difference and Repetition*, New York: Columbia University Press, 1995.

Deleuze, G., *Pourparlers. 1972–1990*, Paris: Les Éditions de Minuit, 1990; trans. M. Joughin, *Negotiations. 1972–1990*, New York: Columbia University Press, 1995.

Deleuze, G., *Proust et les signes*, Paris: Presses Universitaires de France, 1964; trans. R. Howard, *Proust and Signs. The Complete Text*, Minneapolis: University of Minnesota Press, 2000.

De Maistre, X., *Voyage autour de ma chambre*, Paris: Éditions Flammarion, 2003; trans. S. Sartarelli, *Voyage around My Room: Selected Works of Xavier de Maistre*, New York: New Directions, 1994.

Denis, D., *La muse galante. Poétique de la conversation dans l'œuvre de Madeleine de Scudéry*, Paris: Éditions Honoré Champion, 1997.

De Quincey, T., *The Last Days of Immanuel Kant and Other Writings*, Edinburgh: Adam and Charles Black, 1862.

Diderot, D., and d'Alembert, J. le R., eds., *Encyclopédie ou dictionnaire raisonné des sciences, des arts et des métiers*, 28 vols, Paris: Le Breton, Michel-Antoine David, Laurent Durand, & Antoine-Claude Briasson, 1751–1772.

Diderot, D., *Le Rêve de d'Alembert*, ed. C. Duflo, Paris: Éditions Flammarion, 2002; trans. *D'Alembert's Dream*, in *"Rameau's Nephew" and "D'Alembert's Dream,"* ed. L. Tancock, London: Penguin Classics, 1976.

D'Intino, F., "Il monaco indiavolato. Lo *Zibaldone* e la tentazione faustiana di Leopardi," in *Lo Zibaldone cento anni dopo. Composizione, edizioni, temi*, ed. R. Garbuglia, 2 vols, Florence: Olschki, 2001, vol. 2, 467–523

D'Intino, F., *La caduta e il ritorno: cinque movimenti dell'immaginario romantico leopardiano*, Macerata: Quodlibet, 2019.

Donne, J., *The Sermons of John Donne*, eds. G. Plotter and E. M. Simpson, 10 vols, Berkeley: University of California Press, 1953–1962.

Duttlinger, C., *Attention and Distraction in Modern German Literature, Thought, and Culture*, Oxford: Oxford University Press, 2022.

Ender, E., *Architexts of Memory. Literature, Science, and Autobiography*, Ann Arbor: The University of Michigan Press, 2005.

Escola, M., *La Bruyère I, Brèves questions d'herméneutique*, Paris: Éditions Honoré Champion, 2001.

Ferraris, M., *Anima e iPad*, Parma: Guanda, 2011.

Finn, M., *Figures of the Pre-Freudian Unconscious from Flaubert to Proust*, Cambridge: Cambridge University Press, 2017.

Flaubert, G., *La Tentation de saint Antoine*, version of 1849, Paris: Éditions Conard, 1924.

Flaubert, G., *Lettres à Louise Colet: Correspondance 1846–1851*, Lausanne: Éditions Rencontre, 1964.

Flaubert, G., *Madame Bovary*, Paris: Gallimard, 2001; trans. M. Maudlon, *Madame Bovary: Provincial Manners*, Oxford: Oxford University Press, 2020.

Foucault, M., *Histoire de la folie à l'âge classique*, Paris: Gallimard, 1972; trans. J. Khalfa and J. Murphy, *History of Madness*, London: Routledge, 2006.

Foucault, M., *Maladie mentale et psychologie*, Paris: Presses Universitaires de France, 1954; trans. A. Sheridan, *Mental Illness and Psychology*, Berkeley/Los Angeles/London: University of California, 2008.

Foucault, M., *Les aveux de la chair*, ed. F. Gros, Paris: Gallimard, 2018; trans. R. Hurley, *Confessions of the Flesh*, ed. F. Gros, London: Penguin, 2021.

Freud, S., *The Standard Edition of the Complete Psychological Works of Sigmund Freud*, London: Hogarth Press, 1953–1974.

Frigo, A., *L'évidence du Dieu caché. Introduction à la lecture des* Pensées *de Pascal*, Mont-Saint-Aignan: Presses Universitaires de Rouen et du Havre/CNED, 2015.

Genette, G. "Silences de Flaubert," in *Figures I*, Paris: Seuil, 1966; trans. A. Sheridan, "Flaubert's silences," in *Figures of Literary Discourse*, Oxford: Basic Blackwell Publisher, 1982.

Ginzburg, C., *Miti, emblemi, spie. Morfologia e storia*, Turin: Einaudi, 1986; trans. J. and A. C. Tedeschi, *Clues, Myths, and the Historical Method*, Baltimore: Johns Hopkins University Press, 2013.

Hadot, P., *La citadelle intérieure. Introduction aux Pensées de Marc Aurèle*, Paris: Fayard, 1997; trans. M. Chase, *The Inner Citadel: The Meditations of Marcus Aurelius*, Cambridge, MA/London: Harvard University Press, 2001.

Harcourt, B. E., *Exposed. Desire and Disobedience in the Digital Age*, Cambridge, MA: Harvard University Press, 2015.

Harris, J., *Misanthropy in the Age of Reason. Hating Humanity from Shakespeare to Schiller*, Oxford: Oxford University Press, 2022.

Heckscher, W. S., *Art and Literature. Studies in Relationships*, ed. E. Verheyen, Durham, NC: Duke University Press; Baden-Baden: Verlag Valentin Koerner, 1985.

Heidegger, M., *Sein und Zeit*, Halle: Max Niemeyer, 1927; trans. J. Macquarrie and E. Robinson, *Being and Time*, New York: Harper & Row, 1962.

Heidegger, M., *Die Grundbegriffe der Metaphysik: Welt—Endlichkeit—Einsamkeit*, Frankfurt am Main: V. Klostermann, 1983; trans. W. McNeill and N. Walker, *The Fundamental Concepts of Metaphysics: World, Finitude, Solitude*, Bloomington: Indiana University Press, 1995.

Heidegger, M., *Was ist Metaphysik?*, *Wegmarken*, Frankfurt am Main: V. Klostermann, 1967; trans. *What Is Metaphysics?*, in *Pathmarks*, ed. W. McNeill, Cambridge: Cambridge University Press, 1998.

Hobbes, T., *Leviathan*, ed. J. C. A. Gaskin, Oxford: Oxford University Press, 1998.

Hogg, C., "The King in Trinkets: Madeleine de Scudéry's *Conversations* and the Downsizing of Absolutism," *Journal for Eighteenth-Century Studies* 41 (2018): 355–71.

Howells, R. J., *Playing Simplicity: Polemical Stupidity in the Writing of the French Enlightenment*, Oxford/Bern: Peter Lang, 2002.

James, E. D., *Pierre Nicole, Jansenist and Humanist: A Study of His Thought*, The Hague: Martinus Nijhoff, 1972.

Janet, P., *L'automatisme psychologique*, Paris: Félix Alcan, 1889.

Kant, I., *Anthropology from a Pragmatic Point of View*, ed. R. B. Louden, Cambridge: Cambridge University Press, 2006.

Kempis, T. à (attributed to), *The Imitation of Christ*, trans. A. Croft and H. Bolton, New York: Dover Publications, 2012.

Khalfa, J., "Pascal's Theory of Knowledge," in *The Cambridge Companion to Pascal*, ed. N. Hammond, Cambridge: Cambridge University Press, 2003, 122–42.

La Bruyère, J., *Les Caractères ou Les Mœurs de ce siècle*, ed. A. Adam, Paris: Gallimard, 1975; trans. H. van Laun, *The "Characters" of Jean de La Bruyère*, London: G. Routledge & Sons, 1929.

Lacan, J., "Propos sur la causalité psychique," in *Écrits*, vol. 1, Paris: Seuil, 1966; trans. B. Fink, H. Fink, and R. Grigg, *Ecrits: The First Complete Edition in English*, New York/London: W. W. Norton & Co., 2006.

Le Clézio, J.-M., *L'Extase materielle*, Paris: Gallimard, 1967.

Leibniz, G. W., *New Essays Concerning Human Understanding*, in *Selections*, ed. P. P. Wiener, New York: Charles Scribner's Sons, 1951, 374–75.

Leopardi, G., *Operette morali*, ed. A. Prete, Milan: Feltrinelli, 1992; trans. G. Cecchetti, *Essays and Dialogues*, Berkeley/Los Angeles/London: University of California Press, 1982.

Leopardi, G., *Poesie e prose*, ed. M. A. Rigoni, Milan: Mondadori, 1987.

Leopardi, G. *Discorso di un italiano intorno alla poesia romantica*, ed. O. Besomi, Bellinzona: Edizioni Casagrande, 1998; trans. G. Sims and F. Camilletti, *Leopardi's Discourse on Romantic Poetry*, in F. Camilletti, *Classicism and Romanticism in Italian Literature*, London: Pickering & Chatto, 2013.

Leopardi, G., *Zibaldone*, ed. G. Pacella, 3 vols, Milan: Garzanti, 1991; trans. *Zibaldone: The Notebooks of Leopardi*, eds. M. Caesar and F. D'Intino, London: Penguin, 2013.

Leopardi, G., *Epistolario*, eds. Franco Brioschi and Patrizia Landi, Turin: Bollati, 1998.

Locke, J., *An Essay Concerning Human Understanding*, ed. R. S. Woolhouse, London/New York: Penguin, 1997.

Luckhurst, N., *Science and Structure in Proust's* À la recherche du temps perdu, Oxford: Oxford University Press, 2000.

Luhmann, N., *The Reality of the Mass Media*, trans. K. Cross, Stanford: Stanford University Press, 2000.

Maine de Biran, *Journal*, ed. H. Gouhier, 3 vols, Neuchâtel: Éd. De la Baconnière, 1954–1957.

Maine de Biran, *Nouvelles considérations sur le sommeil, les songes et le somnambulisme*, in *Œuvres*, 13 vols, Paris: Vrin, 1984–2001, vol. 5, *Discours à la Société médicale de Bergerac*, ed. F. Azouvi, 1984, 82–123.

Maine de Biran, *De l'aperception immédiate*, ed. A. Devarieux, Paris: Librairie Générale Française, 2005; trans. M. Sinclair, *Of Immediate Apperception*, eds. A. Aloisi, M. Piazza, and M. Sinclair, London/New York: Bloomsbury, 2020.

Manzoni, A., *I promessi sposi*, Milan: Feltrinelli, 2003; trans. *The Betrothed*, London: Lambert & Co., 1856.

Marder, E., *Dead Time: Temporal Disorders in the Wake of Modernity (Baudelaire and Flaubert)*, Stanford: Stanford University Press, 2001.

Marno, D., *Death Be Not Proud: The Art of Holy Attention*, Chicago/London: The University of Chicago Press, 2017.

McKenna, A., *De Pascal à Voltaire. Le rôle des* Pensées *de Pascal dans l'histoire des idées entre 1670 et 1734*, 2 vols, Oxford: Voltaire Foundation, 1990.

Melchior-Bonnet, S., *Une histoire de la frivolité*, Paris: Librairie Armand Colin, 2013.

Menin, M., *Il libro mai scritto. La morale sensitiva di Rousseau*, Bologna: Il Mulino, 2013.

Mesnard, J., "De la 'diversion' au 'divertissement'," in *Mémorial du Premier Congrès International des Études Montaignistes*, Bordeaux: Taffard, 1964, 123–8.

Minardi, M., "Morelli, Berenson, Proust. 'The Art of Connoisseurship'," *Studi di Memofonte* 14 (2015): 211–26.

Montaigne, M. de, *Les Essais*, 3 vols, eds. V.-L. Saulnier and P. Villey, Paris: Presses Universitaires de France, 2004; trans. M. A. Screech, *The Complete Essays*, London: Penguin, 2003.

Morelli, G., *Italian Painters*, trans. C. J. Ffoulkes, London: John Murray, 1892–1893.

Nicole, P., *Continuation des Essais de Morale*, Paris: Guillaume Desprez, 1755.

North, P., *The Problem of Distraction*, Stanford: Stanford University Press, 2012.

Pascal, B., *Pensées*, ed. P. Sellier, Paris: Bordas, coll. "Classiques Garnier," 1991; trans. H. Levi, *Pensées and Other Writings*, ed. A. Levi, Oxford and New York: Oxford University Press, 1995.

Pettnam, D., *Infinite Distraction. Paying Attention to Social Media*, Cambridge: Polity Press, 2016.

Phillips, N. M., *Distraction: Problems of Attention in Eighteenth-Century Literature*, Baltimore: The Johns Hopkins University Press, 2016.

Piaget, J., *La formation du symbole chez l'enfant: imitation, jeu et rêve, image et représentation*, Paris: Delachaux et Niestlé, 1945; trans. *Play, Dreams and Imitation in Childhood*, New York: W.W. Norton & Co., 1962.

Piazza, M., *Il governo di sé. Tempo, corpo e scrittura in Maine de Biran*, Milan: Edizioni Unicopli, 2001.

Piazza, M., "Fra camere e torri, in vista di se stessi. Maine de Biran, Xavier de Maistre e Henri Beyle," in *I viaggi dei filosofi*, eds. M. Bettetini and S. Poggi, Milan: Cortina, 2010, 159–76.

Piazza, M., *Il fantasma dell'interiorità. Breve storia di un concetto controverso*, Milan: Mimesis, 2012.

Piazza, M., *L'antagonista necessario. La filosofia francese dell'abitudine da Montaigne a Deleuze*, Milan: Mimesis, 2015.

Piazza, M., *Creature dell'abitudine. Abito, costume, seconda natura da Aristotele alle scienze cognitive*, Bologna: Il Mulino, 2018.

Plass, P., "Augustine and Proust on Time and Memory," *Soundings: An Interdisciplinary Journal* 73, n. 2/3 (1990): 343–60.

Poincaré, P., *La valeur de la science*, Paris: Éditions Flammarion, 1905; trans. G. B. Halsted, *The Value of Science*, in *The Foundations of Science: Science and Hypothesis, The Value of Science, Science and Method*, Cambridge: Cambridge University Press, 2015.

Poincaré, H., *Science et méthode*, Paris: Éditions Flammarion, 1908; trans. G. B. Halsted, *Science and Method*, in *The Foundations of Science: Science and Hypothesis, The Value of Science, Science and Method*, Cambridge: Cambridge University Press, 2015.

Proust, M., "Impressions de route en automobile," in *Écrits sur l'art*, ed. J. Picon, Paris: Éditions Flammarion, 1999, 249–55.

Proust, M., *À la recherche du temps perdu*, 7 vols, Paris: Gallimard, 1987–1989; trans. *In Search of Lost Time*, trans. C. K. Scott Moncrieff and T. Kilmartin, revisited by D. J. Enring, 6 vols, New York: The Modern Library, 2003.

Proust, M., "Sur la lecture," in *Écrits sur l'art*, ed. J. Picon, Paris: Éditions Flammarion, 1999, 187–224; trans. D. Searls, *On Reading*, London: Hesperus Press Limited, 2011.

Raymond, M., *Romantisme et rêverie*, Paris: José Corti, 1978.

Rancière, J., *L'inconscient esthétique*, Paris: Galilée, 2001; trans. D. Keats and J. Swenson, *The Aesthetic Unconscious*, Cambridge: Polity Press, 2009.

Rancière, J., *Politique de la littérature*, Paris: Galilée, 2007; trans. J. Rose, *The Politics of Literature*, Cambridge: Polity Press, 2011.

Rancière, J., *Le spectateur émancipé*, Paris: La Fabrique, 2008; trans. G. Elliott, *The Emancipated Spectator*, London: Verso, 2011.

Rancière, J., *Aisthesis. Scènes du régime esthétique de l'art*, Paris: Galilée, Paris 2011; trans. Z. Paul, *Aisthesis. Scenes from the Aesthetic Regime of Art*, London/New York: Verso, 2013.

Ribot, T., *Psychologie de l'attention*, Pais: Félix Alcan, Paris, 1889; trans. *The Psychology of Attention*, authorized translation, London: Longmans, Green, & Co., 1890.

Roberts, G. G., "Hugo Gernsback," in *American Magazine Journalists, 1900–1960*, ed. S. G. Riley, Detroit, MI.: Gale Research, 1994, 96–103.

Rousseau, J.-J., *Les Confessions*, eds. B. Gagnebin, M. Raymond, and C. Koenig, Paris: Gallimard, 1959; trans. C. Kelly, *The Confessions and Correspondence, Including the Letters to Malesherbes*, eds. C. Kelly, R. D. Masters, and P. G. Stillman, Hanover and London: University Press of New England, 1995.

Rousseau, J.-J., *Les Rêveries du promeneur solitaire*, ed. É. Leborgne, Paris: Éditions Flammarion, 1997; trans. R. Goulbourne, *Reveries of the Solitary Walker*, Oxford: Oxford University Press 2022.

Saint-Amand, P., *The Pursuit of Laziness. An Idle Interpretation of the Enlightenment*, Princeton/Oxford: Princeton University Press, 2011.

Saint-Évremond, C. de, *Œuvres en prose*, ed. R. Ternois, 4 vols, Paris: Didier, 1962–1969; trans. *The Works of Monsieur de St. Évremond*, London: John Churchill, 1714.

Sand, G., *Histoire de ma vie*, Paris: Gallimard, 2004; trans. *Story of My Life: The Autobiography of George Sand*, ed. T. Jurgrau, Albany, NY: State University of New York Press, 1991.

Schiller, F., *On Grace and Dignity*, in *Schiller's "On Grace and Dignity" in Its Cultural Context: Essays and a New Translation*, eds. J. V. Curran and C. Fricker, Suffolk: Boydell & Brewer, 2005.

Scholar, R., *The Je-Ne-Sais-Quoi in Early Modern Europe. Encounters with a Certain Something*, Oxford: Oxford University Press, 2005.

Scholar, R., *Émigrés: French Words That Turned English*, Princeton, NJ: Princeton University Press, 2020.

Scudéry, M. de, *Conversations nouvelles sur divers sujets*, Paris: Claude Barbin, 1684.

Sellier, P., *Pascal et Saint Augustin*, Paris: Librairie Armand Colin, 1995.

Spinoza, B., *The Correspondence of Spinoza*, ed. A. Wolf., London: George Allen & Unwin, 1928.

Spinoza, B., *Principles of Cartesian Philosophy*, trans. H. E. Wedeck, New York: Philosophical Library, 2014.

Stendhal, *Vie de Henry Brulard*, ed. B. Didier, Paris: Gallimard, 1973; trans. J. Stewart, *The Life of Henry Brulard*, London: Penguin, 1995.

Stendhal, *De l'Amour*, ed. V. Del Litto, Paris: Gallimard, 1980; trans. G. and S. Sale, *Love*, London: Penguin, 2004.

Svevo, I., *La coscienza di Zeno*, Milan: Feltrinelli, 1993; trans. B. de Zoete, *Confessions of Zeno*, London: Putnam, 1930.

Taine, H., *De l'intelligence*, Paris: Librairie Hachette, 1870; trans. T. D. Haye and revised by the author, *On Intelligence*, London: Savill, Edwards and Co., Printers, 1871.

Thomas Neely, C., *Distracted Subjects. Madness and Gender in Shakespeare and Early Modern Culture*, Ithaca, NY: Cornell University Press, 2004.

Tunstall, K. E., "The Early Modern Embodied Mind and the Entomological Imaginary," in *Mind, Body, Motion, Matter: Eighteenth-Century British and French Literary Perspectives*, eds. M. E. McMurran and A. Conway, Toronto: University of Toronto Press, 2016, 202–29.

Van Zuylen, M., *The Plenitude of Distraction*, New York: Sequence Press, 2017.
Voltaire, "Le Mondain", ed. H. T. Mason, in *Œuvres complètes de Voltaire*, vol. 16, Oxford: Voltaire Foundation, 2003, 273–313.
Voltaire, *Lettres philosophiques,* ed. F. Deloffre, Paris: Gallimard, 1986; trans. P. L. Steiner, *Philosophical Letters. Or, Letters Regarding the English Nation*, ed. J. Leigh, Indianapolis/Cambridge: Hackett Publishing Company, 2007.
Voltaire, *Dictionnaire philosophique*, 2 vols, in *Œuvres complètes de Voltaire*, vol. 35:36, ed. C. Mervaud, Oxford: Voltaire Foundation, 1994; trans. J. Fletcher, *A Pocket Philosophical Dictionary*, ed. N. Cronk, Oxford: Oxford University Press, 2011.
Voltaire, "De la frivolité", in *Nouveaux mélanges (1765)*, in *Œuvres complètes de Voltaire*, vol. 60A, ed. N. Cronk, Oxford: Voltaire Foundation, 2017.
Weil, S., *La condition ouvrière*, Paris: Gallimard, 1951.
Weil, S. *La pesanteur et la grâce*, Paris: Plon, 1947; trans. E. Craufurd, *Gravity and Grace*, London: Routledge and Kegan Paul, 1952.
Westfahl, G., *The Mechanics of Wonder. The Creation of the Idea of Science Fiction*, Liverpool: Liverpool University Press, 1998.
Williams, H., *Rousseau and Romantic Autobiography*, Oxford: Oxford University Press, 1983.
Wind, E., *Art and Anarchy*, Evanston, IL: Northwestern University Press, 1985.
Wood, M., *Habits of Distraction*, Brighton: Sussex Academic, 2011.
Wythoff, G., *The Perversity of Things: Hugo Gernsback on Media, Tinkering, and Scientifiction*, Minneapolis, MN: University of Minnesota Press, 2016.
Zolla, E., *Storia del fantasticare*, Milan: Bompiani, 1964.

Index

Adorno, Theodor 171n5
Agamben, Giorgio 141n14, 142n18, 145n3, 152n5
Aloisi, Alessandra 150n4, 152n7
Archimedes 64, 121, 167n8
Aristotle 29, 142n14, 172n4
Arpe, Elena Sofia 142n18
Augustine of Hippo 13, 26, 49, 57, 58, 59, 62–63, 76, 141n13, 151n1, 153n3, 153n4, 154n6, 155n7, 158n5

Bachelard, Gaston 163n5
Balzac, Honoré de 15, 79, 80
Barnwell, Harry Thomas 149n6
Barthes, Roland 126, 143n7, 169n12
Baudelaire, Charles 11, 14, 35, 38, 109, 132, 149n8, 149n9, 164n9, 166n16, 171n3
Becker, Oskar 142n18
Beistegui, Miguel de 146n6, 160n3
Benjamin, Walter 75, 142n15, 157n4, 171n5
Bergson, Henri 14, 15, 77, 79, 80, 84, 98, 105, 116, 118, 122, 126, 128, 130, 135–137, 140n, 143n, 158n9, 158n12, 159n16, 163n7, 165n6, 166n2, 167n5, 167n9, 169n12, 170n4, 170n5, 171n11, 171n13, 172n1, 172n4
Black Mirror 90–93
Blumenberg, Hans 172n3
Bodei, Remo 162n3, 163n9
Boden, Margaret Ann 155n2
Bongiovanni Bertini, Mariolina 159n19
Boullier, Dominique 170n3
Bovary, Emma (character in Flaubert's *Madame Bovary*) 101, 120, 132, 167n6

Bowlby, Rachel 162n3
Bray, Patrick 157n3, 161n8
Breaking Bad 9
Brilli, Attilio 165n3
Brun, Jean 145n2
Bucknall, Barbara 158n5
Burton, Robert 13, 143n1
Butler, Samuel 110, 166n3

Cabanis, Pierre-Jean-Georges 11, 68, 70, 71, 72, 75, 156n2
Calzolari, Olmo 165n9
Camilletti, Fabio 163n6, 167n6
Campo, Enrico 139n6
Caranfa, Angelo 158n5
Carboni, Massimo 142n20
Carnevali, Barbara 165n2
Carraud, Vincent 145n2
Cassian, John 66
Certeau, Michel de 146n2
Chabaneix, Paul 71–72, 75, 156n1, 157n9
Chaplin, Charlie 142n17
Citton, Yves 4, 18, 129, 144n10, 144n11, 170n8, 171n2
Cléro, Jean-Pierre 149n4
Coccia, Emanuele 152n5
Coleridge, Samuel Taylor 98
Colerus, Johannes 62, 154n2
Colet, Louise 102
Condillac, Étienne Bonnot de 61, 68, 70, 110, 154n1, 156n6, 166n1
Condorcet, Jean-Antoine-Nicolas, marquis de 147n3
Corot, Camille 130
Crary, Jonathan 6, 140n11
Cristofolini, Paolo 154n3

Index

d'Alembert, Jean-Baptiste Le Rond 22, 71, 124, 145n4, 169n8
See also : *Encyclopédie*
Darmon, Jean-Charles 147n4, 149n5
Delacroix, Eugène 121
Deleuze, Gilles, 17, 26, 28, 75, 85, 128, 131, 141n, 144n 147, 154n4, 157n6, 157n3, 161n2, 170n6, 171n14
Denis, Delphine 149n2
Descartes, René 36, 71, 124, 141, 168n4
De Quincey, Thomas 102, 164n11
Diderot, Denis 22, 67, 70–71, 95, 97, 124, 125, 145n4, 155n7, 157n7, 162n3, 163n4, 169n8, 169n9
See also : *Encyclopédie*
Diogenes Laërtius 147n9
D'Intino, Franco 151n6, 166n5
Donne, John 153n1, 158
Don Quixote (character in Cervantes's *Don Quixote*) 124, 126, 127, 135
Dreyer, Carl Theodor 9
Duttlinger, Carolin 142n15

Encyclopédie 124, 126–127, 145n4, 155n7, 162n3, 168n2, 169n8, 170n1
Ender, Evelyne 158n8
Escola, Marc 170–171n10

Facebook 22
Ferraris, Maurizio 152n2
Finn, Michael 157n8
Flaubert, Gustave 101–102, 164n7
See also: Bovary, Emma (character in Flaubert's *Madame Bovary*)
Fontenelle, Bernard Le Bovier de 28
Foucault, Michel 125, 132, 155n5, 168n1, 169n10, 171n1
Franklin, Benjamin 68
Freud, Sigmund 11, 15, 82–83, 114, 115, 159n20, 159n21, 160n22, 160n23, 160n24, 160n26, 162–163n3, 166n1
Frigo, Alberto 151n2

Genette, Gérard 101, 164n8
Gernsback, Hugo 1–3, 5, 139n1
Ginzburg, Carlo 159n15, 160n22
Goethe, Johann Wolfgang von 71

Hadot, Pierre 151n7
Harcourt, Bernard 144n9
Harris, Joseph 147n2, 172n4
Heckscher, William Sebastian 155n8
Hegel, Georg Wilhelm Friedrich 71
Heidegger, Martin 13, 21, 23, 100, 142n15, 142n18, 145n2, 145–146n6, 146n7, 164n5
Heraclitus 125
Hobbes, Thomas 69, 156n3
Hogg, Chloé 148n2
Horkheimer, Max 171n5
Howell, James 169n5
Howells, Robin 149n1
Hsieh, Tehching 165n7

James, Edward D. 145n5, 155n1
James, William 110
Janet, Pierre 117, 119, 167n4, 167n1, 167n2

Kafka, Franz 142n15
Kant, Immanuel 11, 65–66, 103, 155n4, 161n1
Karenina, Anna (character in Tolstoj's *Anna Karenina*) 167n6
Khalfa, Jean 149n4
Kracauer, Siegfried 171n5

La Bruyère, Jean de 14, 35, 38, 125, 129, 148n1, 162n2, 167n3, 169n11, 170n10
See also: Ménalque

Lacan, Jacques 168n4
La Fayette, Madame de (Marie-Madeleine Pioche de La Vergne) 23
La Fontaine, Jean de 71
Laurel and Hardy (Stan Laurel and Oliver Hardy, comedy duo) 127
Le Clézio, Jean-Marie Gustave 9, 142n19
Leibniz, Gottfried Wilhelm von 44, 118, 167–168n11
Leopardi, Giacomo 14, 44, 51–54, 150n5, 151n1, 151n2, 151n3, 151n5, 151n6, 158n10, 161n1, 163n6, 165n3, 165n9, 166n13, 167n3, 172n4
Le Roy, Georges 156n6
Locke, John 11, 37, 43, 69–71, 96, 98, 103, 124, 156n4, 169n6
Luckhurst, Nicola 157n1
Luhmann, Niklas 171n5

Maine de Biran, François-Pierre Gontier 25, 40–46, 110, 119–120, 129, 150n2, 150n5, 150n3, 150n4, 156n2, 165n10, 167n4, 167n5, 170n7
Maistre, Joseph de 112
Maistre, Xavier de 112, 113–115, 165n10
Manet, Édouard 120
Manzoni, Alessandro 120, 167n
Marcus Aurelius 45–46, 151n
Marder, Elissa 140n
Marker, Chris 137
Marno, David 140n8, 140n13, 147n5, 153n1
McKenna, Antony 148n7
Melchior-Bonnet, Sabine 148n6
Ménalque (potrait in La Bruyère's *Caractères*) 9, 95, 117, 121, 125–126, 129–130, 142n15, 168n, 169n13, 170n9, 171n9

Menin, Marco 150n2
Mesnard, Jean 146n1
Minardi, Mauro 159n15
Montaigne, Michel Eyquem de 10, 14, 24–28, 31, 36, 38, 42, 43, 53, 54, 60, 61, 146n2, 146n3, 147n9, 152n1
Morelli, Giovanni (Nicolas Schäffer) 80, 159n15, 160n22
Mozart, Wolfgang Amadeus 71

Newton, Isaac 64
Nicole, Pierre 23, 63, 145n5, 155n1
Nietzsche, Friedrich Wilhelm 26
North, Paul 141–142n15, 169n13

Pascal, Blaise 5–6, 10, 13, 14, 18, 21–24, 25–30, 31–36, 38, 39, 40–42, 144–145n1, 145n2, 145n5, 147n2, 149n3, 149n1, 151n4, 168n4
Pettman, Dominic 139n5
Phillips, Natalie M. 155n7
Piaget, Jean 99, 163n1
Piazza, Marco 149n7, 150n5, 150n3, 157n, 165n10, 166n2
Petrarch (Francesco Petrarca) 153n1
Plass, Paul 158n5
Plato 29, 172n3
Plutarch 167n8
Poe, Edgar Allan 139n
Poincaré, Henri 10, 63, 64–68, 72–73, 74–75, 155n3, 155n6, 157n10
Prete, Antonio 151n1
Proust, Marcel 2, 3, 4, 9, 11, 14, 15, 16, 61, 63, 74–79, 81–90, 101, 104–105, 123, 143n6, 153n6, 154n1, 157n8, 157n2, 157n3, 158n5, 158n6, 158n8, 159n13, 159n15, 159n17, 159n18, 159n19, 160n22, 160n1, 161n1, 161n4, 161n5, 161n7, 161n1, 164n6, 167n7, 167n10

Rancière, Jacques 107, 129, 160n25, 161n6, 164n7, 166n11, 170n8, 171n5
Ravaisson, Félix 110
Raymond, Marcel 163n3
Régis, Emmanuel 71, 157n9
Regnard, Jean-François 172n4
Ribot, Théodule-Armand 14, 143n3
Roberts, Garyn G. 139n1
Rousseau, Jean-Jacques 11, 14, 43–44, 46, 103–109, 150n1, 154n1, 164n1, 165n2, 165n5, 165n7, 166n1, 166n14, 166n15
Ruskin, John 143n6

Saint-Amand, Pierre 146n2, 154n1, 165n8
Saint-Évremond, Charles de Marguetel de Saint-Denis, sieur de 38, 149n6
Sand, George (Aurore Dupin) 14, 99–100, 101, 164n4
Schiller, Friedrich 71, 80, 159n14
Scholar, Richard 145n4, 148n2, 150n6
Schopenhauer, Arthur 71
Scott, Sir Walter 71
Sellier, Philippe 147n5
Sévigné, Marie de Rabutin-Chantal, marquise de 23
Sévigné, Renaud de, Comte de Montmoron 23
Socrates 70
Sorel, Julien (character in Stendhal's *Le Rouge et le Noir*) 107, 132, 167n6
Spinoza, Baruch 10, 26, 28, 62, 154n5
Staël, Madame de (Anne-Louise-Germaine Necker) 71
Stendhal (Marie-Henri Beyle) 11, 15–16, 85, 107, 143n5, 160n2, 165n10
See also: Sorel, Julien (character in Stendhal's *Le Rouge et le Noir*)

Svevo, Italo (Aron Hector Schmitz) 112, 166n4

Taine, Hyppolite 98, 163n8, 170n7
Tandello, Emanuela 165n9
Tarde, Gabriel 18
Tati, Jacques (Jacques Tatischeff) 129
The Imitation of Christ 56, 152n3, 152n4
Thirouin, Laurent 149n3
Thomas à Kempis 152n3
See also: *The Imitation of Christ*
Thomas Neely, Carol 169n5
Thomas Aquinas 63
Tolstoj, Lev 71
See also: Karenina, Anna (character in Tolstoj's *Anna Karenina*)
Tunstall, Kate 156n8
Turner, William 130

van Zuylen, Marina 140n7
Verne, Jules 139n1
Voltaire (François-Marie Arouet) 14, 28–32, 35–41, 43, 71, 124, 147n1, 147n3, 148n4, 148n5, 148n6, 149n, 168n3, 169n

Walpole, Horace 62
Warman, Caroline 165n9
Weil, Simone 7–8, 88, 142n16, 142n17, 161n3
Wells, Herbert George 139n1
Wenders, Wim 57
Westfahl, Gary 139n1
Williams, Huntington 162n1
Wind, Edgar 159n15
Wood, Michael 143n7, 158n8
Wythoff, Grant 139n1

Zabunyan, Dork 171n5
Zolla, Elemir 153n4, 167n6

www.ingramcontent.com/pod-product-compliance
Lightning Source LLC
Chambersburg PA
CBHW052120300426
44116CB00010B/1732